Krešimir Šeg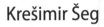

A CONVERSATION WITH
THE VISIONARIES

Medjugorje 2014

IT ALL BEGAN IN THE EVENING HOURS OF JUNE 24, 1981

Four girls and two boys saw a beautiful vision with a Child in Her hands.

The first to see this vision were Ivanka Ivanković and Mirjana Dragićević, then later Vicka Ivanković, Milka Pavlović, Ivan Dragićević and Ivan Pavlović.

The next day, on June 25th, at the same time - at about 6 pm - at the same place on Podbrdo above Bijakovići, Ivanka, Mirjana, Ivan Dragićević and Vicka came.

Suddenly a light flashed. The children saw an indescribably beautiful apparition – the Gospa (as Our Lady is called in Croatian) – but this time without the Child in Her hands.

Vicka ran down to the hamlet Bijakovići and brought back with her Milka's sister Marija and little Jakov Čolo. Milka and Ivan Ivanković, who were present the day before, were not there.

From that second day on, Ivanka, Mirjana, Ivan, Vicka, Marija and Jakov would become overjoyed visionaries – *angels of the Gospa.*

From then on, they will be the ones to whom the Gospa will appear, through whom She will speak to the parish of Medjugorje and to the rest of the world, through whom She will call for peace, for conversion, for the strengthening of faith through prayer and fasting.

The news spread throughout the region with the speed of light. On the fifth day of the apparitions, there were already 15.000 devout and inquisitive people gathered on Apparition Hill.

Despite the resistance of the communist government, despite the prohibition to visit the apparition site, despite the threats and intimidations as well as the imprisonment of the parish priest (who, at first, did not believe in the apparitions himself), the number of pilgrims grew from day to day. They came from all over, from near and far - from Bosnia and Herzegovina, Croatia, Slovenia, then from Italy, Germany and other European countries. Then pilgrims followed from North and South America, from Africa, Asia and Australia.

People of all ages and classes came, men and women, wealthy and impoverished alike, priests, bishops, archbishops and cardinals.

Medjugorje grew into the new spiritual center of the world - the words of Pope John Paul II himself.

According to the decision of the Bishops' Conference of former Yugoslavia and the clear standpoint of Cardinal Josef Ratzinger, then Prefect of the Congregation of the Doctrine of the Faith and today Pope Benedict XVI, Medjugorje became the spiritual meeting site, which attracted the highest amount of attention.

In the beginning, the local ordinary defended the visionaries and said that they were speaking the truth. Later, he and his successor did not accept the apparitions as being authentic. However, they do not prohibit the gathering of the faithful nor do they refuse them their sacraments.

The Church has not made its final decision. The apparitions are still going on and, as long as this is so, the Church - as Mother and Teacher - watches all events closely.
Time is not an issue.
In the meantime, the faithful keep coming and are already coming for 30 years.

I, myself, on the other hand, cannot but believe in the reality of Medjugorje.
My thoughts are there night and day.
I read and gather everything about the events and translate beautiful testimonies from all languages:
God is acting through the Gospa in Medjugorje.
I abide only by the criteria of Jesus:
"The tree is known by its fruits."
And those fruits are: encounters with God, with the Eucharistic Jesus and with the Gospa.
All pilgrims return home with the same wish to return again and with the same decision:
If we live the messages of the Gospa, we build a better world on the basis of the gospel.

Msgr. Eduard Peričić

(Msgr. Eduard Peričić is a member of the International Marian Academy and confessor of His Holiness, priest of the Zadar archdiocese and professor who regularly visits Medjugorje on the second of every month. The fruits of his pilgrimages and his research on the Medjugorje spiritual phenomenon are imparted in several published books. His lyrical thoughts are part of his new book, which is in preparation).

Ivanka Ivanković-Elez

The first to see the Woman with the Child in Her hands on Podbrdo on June 24, 1981 was Ivanka Ivanković-Elez, born on the 21st of June 1966. The Gospa appeared to her every day until May 7, 1985, when the 10th secret was revealed to her. Since then, the Gospa has been appearing to her once a year - on the anniversary of the apparitions - the 25th of June. During the daily apparitions, the Gospa told Ivanka of Her life and continues to do so during the annual apparitions. Ivanka will publish the Gospa's bibliography when She grants her permission to do so.

Ivanka lives in the village of Miletina in the parish of Medjugorje. She is married to Rajko and they have three children – Kristina, Josip and Ivo.

Her special intention is to pray for families.

ALL YOU NEED IS TO OPEN
YOUR HEART TO THE GOSPA

Can you tell me why the anniversary is being celebrated on the 25ᵗʰ and not on the 24ᵗʰ of June when you first saw the Gospa?

On the first day of the apparitions we were frightened and ran away. Therefore, our first real meeting with the Gospa, when we talked and prayed together, was on the 25ᵗʰ. The Gospa Herself said that the anniversaries were to be celebrated on June 25ᵗʰ.

All the visionaries testify that they await each apparition with impatience at 6.40 pm. You had daily apparitions for four years. After that, the impatience before this great event that had determined your life came to a sudden stop. But it still influences your life. What I am asking is: Was it strange for you when the time of the apparition came but the Gospa did not appear?

It was difficult to accept that the Gospa was no longer going to appear to me every single day, as She had done up to May 7, 1985. The feeling of emptiness that I felt for a long time after that cannot be described - the time of the apparition would soon arrive but the Gospa would not appear to me. Through prayer, I managed to accept that this was God's will and that this was how it was supposed to be. During the apparition on May 7ᵗʰ, the Gospa said: *"Do not be sad. I will be coming to you on every anniversary, except this one. My child, do not think that you have done something wrong and that that is the reason why I will not be appearing to you anymore. No, you have done nothing wrong! You embraced and executed all the plans my Son and I had. Be happy because I am your Mother and I love you with all my heart. Ivanka, thank you for following the call my Son with such perseverance and for always being with Him when He requested that of you."*

During the time of the apparition, my family and I pray the rosary every day, and we thank the Gospa for all the graces and gifts that I, my family, the parish and the world have received.

Are the annual apparitions in any way different from the daily apparitions?
The annual apparitions are the same as the daily apparitions that I had until May 7, 1985. The Gospa visits me in the same manner; She is equally beautiful and joyful. She greets me with *"Praised be Jesus Christ"* and gives me a message. Before the Gospa appears, I see a bright flash of light that repeats itself three times. Then we pray together and She gives Her motherly blessing. When She appears on the anniversary, She is always dressed exactly as I have described Her during my last regular apparition: *Her dress and especially Her crown glimmer in silver and gold.*

The Gospa told you about Her life. Did She finish this, and when will the story of Her life be published?
During last year's apparition, the Queen of Peace also told me of Her life, which means that She has not finished yet. How long this will be I do not know.

Can you tell our readers anything about what you have written so far?

No. I will be able to do so only when the Gospa grants me permission.

How do you prepare for the annual apparitions?

The preparations last the whole year, beginning with the 25th of June. I prepare myself through daily prayer and daily activities. About two weeks before the apparition takes place, I prepare by fasting and praying. The closer the apparition comes, the stronger becomes my yearning to see the Gospa. Then every single moment seems to last a year, the days seem to pass very slowly.

Do you ever tell the Gospa about your private life?

I have never asked the Gospa for anything concerning my private life; since Her apparition is a gift in itself and it would be inappropriate to ask for something for myself.

Mirjana, Jakov and you have all already received the ten secrets. Do these secrets that have been unveiled to you only concern the future of the world or do some secrets concern only your life?

All the secrets I have received concern the future of the world. The third secret concerns the sign that the Gospa will leave on Apparition Hill. The sign will be permanent, visible for all and indestructible.

Have you seen the sign?

I have seen the sign and I know when it will occur. But we should not wait with our conversion until this day. We need to convert every day, we need *to live* the messages the Gospa has been giving us for the last 27 years.

13

All you need to do is open your heart to the Gospa, She will take care of the rest. A person, who lives far away from God, thinks that the goal of life lies in material things - to always want to have more and to attain more - but the Gospa wishes that we answer Her call and She wishes to lead us closer to Her Son Jesus every day. This cannot happen if one does not have an open heart, if one does not pray, repent and fast. We need to finally understand what a grace it is that the sky opens here every day and that the Mother of God comes and wants to lead us on the path of holiness.

The Gospa is always with us and She wishes to teach us that the goal of our life is Heaven, eternal life. Already at the beginning of the apparitions, I was able to see this eternal life when the Queen of Peace allowed me to see my mother, who had died a month before the first apparition.

Do you know when and how you will reveal the ten secrets? Mirjana will do this through Fr. Petar Ljubičić and she also described how we should prepare for this.
I do not know anything about this; therefore, I cannot say anything about it. It will be as the Blessed Virgin wishes it to be.

On June 24, 1981, you and Mirjana went for a walk on Podbrdo when you suddenly saw a Woman with an Infant. What did you think at first?
First of all, we were overwhelmed with fear, a terrible fear. Despite this fear, I felt in my heart that this could be the Gospa and I immediately said this to Mirjana. Our first impulse was to run away, but we returned soon thereafter and saw the Gospa again. Since the 25th of June, the Gospa continued to appear to Mirjana, Vicka, Ivan, Marija, Jakov and me.

Have you ever asked the Gospa why She chose to appear to you?

Yes and She answered that She does not choose the best.

The apparitions have now been taking place for twenty seven years. This gives some people reason to doubt their authenticity. Did you ever ask the Gospa why She is appearing for so long?

In the beginning, we were persuaded by others to ask Her how long She would be appearing. This is what the Gospa answered: *"Are you tired of me already?"* Since then, I have never asked Her anything similar. When speaking about the time and the number of apparitions of the Gospa in Medjugorje, I would like to say that, in the end, only our dear Lord and His Mother, who love us deeply, know what is best for us. Today, there are so many cold hearts in the world, there is so much sin and so much evil; therefore, we should not be surprised by God's efforts and the Gospa's patience.

On many occasions, the Gospa told us that She is with us because God has allowed Her to do so and that She will stay with us for as long as He allows it.

What about the fruits of Medjugorje?

Others will have more to say on this subject; for example, the priests who hear confession for hours in our church, in the confessionals and on the nearby lawn. When meeting with pilgrims, I frequently hear testimonies of conversion, of spiritual and physical healings that occurred because of the intercession of the Queen of Peace. Here, people feel better, they feel the need to change their life.

Once when I went to Sicily to attend a prayer meeting, I met a 22-year-old man, who had cancer. He was severely ill and he wanted to visit Medjugorje. So he did. His parents, his fiancé and I travelled to Medjugorje together by car. He attended holy Mass in the church, he climbed Cross Mountain and was as happy as a child. He cried continuously. During those few days, his whole life changed completely. He felt peace that he had never experienced before. Then, he returned home and died seven days later.

Later, his parents wrote me and told me what those days in Medjugorje had meant for them and their son. His death was difficult for them to cope with but they understood what God expected of them. They changed their life, they went to confession, they again go to church and they started to pray... They realized what the true meaning of their life on earth was. This young man's grandfather, who had not gone to confession for 60 years and had never needed God, also converted. Actually, the whole family experienced a conversion. These are the fruits of Medjugorje.

Another example comes from a nun from America. Before she became a nun, she had spent all her efforts to enhance her career, to make lots of money, she was interested in fashion, jewelry and expensive cars... After being involved in a car accident, she was left blind. During her fight for survival, she came to know God and became a nun. She says that she can never thank God enough for all the gifts she received. One does not have to see the Gospa with one's own eyes, one does not have to be a visionary to see Heaven. What is important is to open one's heart, to pray with the heart. This is what the Gospa always asks of us.

Every visionary prays for a special intention. What is your special intention?

Every day, I pray for the families, for every family in the world, so that they may learn how much God loves them.

We all see how marriages and families are becoming less important, how many divorces there are, how many abandoned children there are, how many abortions there are. Where life should be born, death now prevails. That is why it is necessary to pray constantly and persistently. I would like to take this opportunity to ask all those, who will be reading this, to pray for families here.

Mirjana Dragićević-Soldo

Mirjana Dragićević-Soldo was born on March 18, 1965 in Sarajevo. She had daily apparitions until Christmas of 1982. During this last daily apparition, the Queen of Peace revealed the tenth secret to her and told her that, from then on, She would be appearing to her on the 18th of March for the rest of her life. Since the 2nd of August 1987, Mirjana hears the voice of the Gospa and also sees Her on the second of every month. This apparition is to pray for those who have not yet experienced the love of God.

She lives with her husband Marko and her children Veronika and Marija in Bijakovići near the Podbrdo.

WE ALL RECEIVED GREAT
GRACES THROUGH MEDJUGORJE

Allow me to ask you the following question: We often read or hear questions as to why, of all places, the Gospa chose Bijakovići, the parish of Medjugorje and the six of you for Her apparitions? Soon we will celebrate the 27th anniversary of the apparitions. Can you tell us the answer to this question? Why Bijakovići and why the six of you?

During an apparition, we asked the Gospa why She had chosen our village and the six of us. We asked Her this during the first days of the apparitions. She told us that She had found faith here; this is all She said concerning our question why She chose our village. When we asked Her why She chose the six of us - since we were just like all the other children in the village, not special in any way - the Gospa told us that She chose us because She needed us just the way we were. This is all She ever said concerning us. Honestly, I never think about this because, when you say yes to your Mother, the Mother of God, then you do not have time to think of such things. You put yourself into Her hands because you are safest there, and you know that She only wishes you well when you do - or at least try to do - what She wants of you through prayer, fasting and conversion. You try to do what She asks of you. This is what I try to tell everyone, who comes to Medjugorje and loses time by asking questions such as why and wherefore...? Don't ask why but rather try to follow what God tells us through the Gospa, because this will surely lead to Jesus and to salvation.

The Gospa chose us because of the way we are. In this regard, there is a nice event that took place with the late Fr. Slavko. For a year, he had tried to set up a meeting with the six of us. When he visited me once, he was angry and so I asked him: "Father, what has upset you so?" He answered half angry and half joking: "How can you ask such a thing?! If I were the Gospa, I would never ever have chosen you. But this is a sign that She truly is in Medjugorje because She did choose you."

When you go back to June of 1981 - you were sixteen years old then - did you ever imagine then that the apparitions would last for so long and that they would bring about so many changes in our parish and in the world?

Then, when the apparitions began, I only thought of tomorrow and when I would see Her again. Because seeing Her meant for me being in Heaven. Whenever I speak of this, I always give this example: I have two daughters. They say that motherly love, the love for your own child, is – with the exception of love for God – the most powerful love. However, when I am with the Gospa, I don't even think about my children. Therefore, during those first days of the apparitions, when I did not even know about Lourdes or Fatima or even that the Gospa could appear at all, I didn't think about what would happen. I only had one single wish: *Don't leave us, come back tomorrow.* It was so special to be with Her and still is after all this time.

On the Nativity of St. John the Baptist, on the 24th of June, 1981, Ivanka and you went for a walk. All of a sudden you saw a vision of a Lady with an Infant. When Ivanka said that she saw the Gospa, you did not believe

her and thought: *How on earth could it be that the Gospa appears to us?* **When did you first believe that this was really the Mother of God?**

As I said earlier, up until that point, I didn't even know that the Gospa could come down to earth. Although I prayed the rosary every night and went to Mass on Sundays, I never knew that such things could occur. When Ivanka said that she saw the Gospa, I didn't even look towards the direction she was pointing to. In an angry voice, I even said to her: *"Sure, the Gospa has nothing better to do than to visit you and me."* Our parents had taught us to live according to God's Commandment *not to use God's name in vein,* and now Ivanka was saying that she saw the Gospa up on the hillside. At this moment, in my eyes, Ivanka was a sinner, so I left her and wanted to return to the village. As soon as I came close to the houses at the foot of the hill, I felt such a strong urge from within that I needed to return. When I came back, Ivanka was still standing at the same spot. She then said: *"Please, look now."* Then I saw a Woman in a long grey dress holding a Child in Her arms. Straight away I knew it was the Mother of God because of what came over me then - the joy, the beauty - and even my not understanding where all this came from, how it was possible that I could see Her – I never doubted for a second, I knew that it was Her.

How did it come about that you and Ivanka were walking up the path up Podbrdo? Some say that you went to fetch your sheep, others say that you went for a walk?

Ivanka came from Mostar and I came from Sarajevo. We just wanted to talk like sixteen-year-old girls usually do and confide in one another. It was important for us that no one bothered us and this is why we went for a walk on this side of the village.

Actually, like every summer, you came to Medjugorje for the summer holidays. When did you go back to Sarajevo?

I really didn't want to go back to Sarajevo because I thought that, if I did so, my apparitions would end. However, you also must keep in mind that, back then, we had communist regime and I was forced back to Sarajevo by the police, I was forced to leave Medjugorje. They made me leave. The same day I arrived in Sarajevo, I had an apparition at the same time when the rest of the children in Bijakovići had theirs. The Gospa gave them the same message She gave me in Sarajevo.

Did your life in Sarajevo change, considering that the visionaries and their parents were persecuted? The media said that all of you made the whole thing up and the authorities requested that you stop talking about it.

It was easier here in Medjugorje, as it was one nation and everyone was Catholic. It was different for me because I was alone. Before the apparitions took place, I attended a classical secondary school. It was considered the best of its kind in Sarajevo. As soon as I came back to school, I was expelled and the whole ordeal was accompanied with ugly words. My father managed to transfer me to another school, but this class was attended by all the other students who had been expelled from the other five classical secondary schools in Sarajevo. You can imagine how I felt; the newspapers were full of terrible articles about me. I read that I was the granddaughter of a war criminal and that the Gospa was a fabrication made up by nationalists. But I am a believer and I love all people regardless of their faith. This is what the Gospa teaches us; She tells us that we are all brothers and sisters, that we must all see Jesus Christ in every person.

Every day, I was taken away by officers of the Republic Secretariat of Internal Affairs. They interrogated and questioned me. They demanded that I write and sign a statement that Fr. Jozo Zovko fabricated the whole event which took place in Medjugorje. I was convinced that I needed to speak the truth and I told them that I had never even met Fr. Jozo before. He had become the parish priest at the end of 1980 and I came to Medjugorje for the summer holidays in June of 1981 while Fr. Jozo was in Zagreb. I was persistent in trying to convince them that I did not know Fr. Jozo, but they kept on with their threats and they would repeatedly bring me in for interrogation. It was embarrassing for me to bring an excuse note from the Secretariat to school, as if I was a notorious criminal.

I felt sorry for those who interrogated and threatened me. But, through this ordeal, my parents were extremely helpful to me. They told me to be persistent in telling the truth, that they would stand by me and that God would help us. Truly, so it was. However, I was not the only one who had problems. Actually, my own problems did not matter to me so much, I kept thinking: *I am seeing the Gospa and this is how it is supposed to be.* This comforted me but it was difficult for me to watch my parents and my little brother suffer and cry.

My parents suffered persecution and threats that they would get fired, but God helped us through this all. I truly saw God's work in everything. Doors that I thought would never be opened suddenly opened. When I thought I was all alone there was always someone there to help me. In this, I saw how the Mother of God acts through different people.

Was it then that you came to Medjugorje more often?

I came, but the police kept taking me back to Sarajevo. I remember a very nasty incident. They cursed, they threatened me, they yelled at me and, when they brought me back to my apartment, I said to my mother: "Mom, if you only knew what they put me through." My mother hinted to me with her eyes to keep quiet and not to talk, because it could have been even worse. Everything passes. If something comes from God, nobody can stop it.

Was it difficult for you to be separated from the other visionaries? How did the apparitions continue to take place?

In a way, it was difficult, but no one and nothing is as important as the Mother of God. Only She was important to me, what She said to me and what I was supposed to do. It is nice to be with the rest of the visionaries, but it was important to me to be with Her, to see Her. That is why I did not want to go back to Sarajevo. I thought that, if I left Medjugorje, I would not see Her again and that the apparitions would come to an end. Nothing else mattered.

Considering all the threats that were made and all the ugly words that were directed towards you, was it hard? How did you endure it all?

I was able to endure everything through prayer. I actually felt sorry for these people. While they were cursing, threatening and yelling at me, they acted like characters you see in the movies - they played good guy/bad guy - I somehow learned how to cope with them and how to act. While they were acting their roles, I thought to myself: *My Lord, how unhappy these people must be, how restless they must be, how much pain they must be carrying inside.* I felt that only really unhappy people could act this way towards others, so I prayed for them from my heart. I prayed that God may let them find peace because, when they would find peace, they would change and understand. I was never capable of hating them, never.

The Gospa said that She would finish in Medjugorje what She had started in Fatima. The reactions of the authorities, both secular and Church authorities, were almost identical to the ones in Fatima and Lourdes with regard to the statements that the Gospa had appeared in Medjugorje. Always, the same arguments were made – that the visionaries were fabricating the whole event and that they were lying, that they were talked into doing so, that they were clearly ill... Why such reactions?

I like the fact that our Church is cautious because there are many apparitions reported in the world and, in the end, it turns out that they are not authentic. I was never worried about the fact that the Church is waiting and examining the events because I know what I see. When my Church proves what I see, then the Church will approve what I see. Whenever I think of this, I say to myself: *My dear Gospa, I do what You ask of me; the Church and the priesthood – this is Your responsibility. You know what You have to do about this, I leave this unto You, You guide them.* I let our Heavenly Mother deal with this, She will take care of this.

In the beginning it was difficult for me that people did not believe us and that they were saying that we were making it all up. Gradually, this has stopped, but I feel sorry for those, who continue to think and feel this way, who continuously wonder whether or not this all is true, while the Gospa is stretching out Her hand to lead us to salvation. Why do you waste time? I also often asked myself: *Why should I invent such a lie?* If

I were lying, this would make me an abnormal person. Even during communism, the doctors stated that we were normal. I had a nice life, I lived with my parents as the only child for nine years; they cherished me. Why would I want to turn my life upside down, why bring turmoil, anxiety, agony and pain into my life – why? In my opinion, only an unstable person can do such a thing. It is different now; communism no longer reigns here and neither does the former country exist. Now it is nice to be a visionary, but back then... Why would someone want to do that? I always wanted to ask those, who considered me a liar: "Why should I lie? What would I gain by lying?"

Comparing the apparitions in Medjugorje with the most famous apparitions in the rest of the world, we see similarities but there are also differences: mainly, the number of visionaries, the many messages received, the enormous number of apparitions as well as the duration of the apparitions. Do you understand why the apparitions are still taking place?

In this way, the Gospa is preparing us for everything that is going to take place through the love of God our Father. She said that She would finish in Medjugorje what She has started in Fatima and that Her heart would prevail. She is preparing us for this victory. When these events will begin, people will understand why She chose the 18th of March and why the apparitions take place every second day of the month. They will understand the importance of these dates, why She has been appearing for so long and why so many visionaries.

Do you see any signs of these events being put into motion, are they happening now or are they awaiting us in the far future?

I see small signs, they are already here; slowly, things are starting to move. Women will understand me better with the following example: When we want to do our spring cleaning, we first turn our homes upside down. We move our sofas, cupboards, tables, chairs – nothing remains in its place. To someone it may seem like a mess but, when we put everything back into its place, everything is spick and span. Therefore, if we wish to make some order, we first need to make a big mess. I can see the signs of this.

The basic messages that Our Lady gives in Medjugorje are peace, faith, conversion, prayer and the importance of fasting. Have people understood these messages and can you say that they have not fallen on deaf ears? Does this need to be repeated every single day?

Remembering the first days and my neighbors from Podbrdo, whom I knew best, I can honestly say that they have accepted everything with open hearts. They helped us, hid us and protected us as best they could. They said *yes* to the Gospa. But I feel that we all need to ask ourselves personally to what degree we have answered to the Gospa's calls and how much we do in this sense. I don't like when people talk about other people. I mean that everyone should talk about himself. The Gospa desires of us peace, prayer, fasting, penance... What is important is how often we follow this because, if we do it in the silence of our own homes, we will pass this onto our families, we will pass it on to our neighbors, the village, the country... But this will only happen if we start with ourselves and not with others. It is important how each one of us accepts this and not what others do. I don't think that the Gospa asks of us to pray and fast just for the sake of doing it, I think She asks this of us so that prayer and fasting teach us to love. During one apparition, She said: **"My name is Love! I came here to teach you to do what you have forgotten - to love!"**

Prayer and fasting leads us to this. The most important command that Jesus taught us is to love God, to love others. I think that the Gospa wants us to grow in this sense, to love people, to see Jesus Christ in them. Therefore, I always say that we need to start with ourselves. I do not know how others have embraced this and I do not know how others have answered this call, only our dear Lord knows this. Everybody is responsible for himself. When you and I come before God, He will not ask me how you were, He will ask me how I have answered His call. He will ask you about yourself.

Pope John Paul II said: Medjugorje brings hope to the entire world.

We have all received great gifts in Medjugorje, both spiritual and material. I remember, as a child I used to come here during the summer holidays, I remember how people used to live before the apparitions and how we all have risen along with the Gospa and Her bread. We should all be thankful to our dear Mother for this through our actions and not only through our words. This means that all the pilgrims, who come here, feel like they have come home to their own mother, that they see the Gospa and Her messages in each and everyone of us. Not that - and I really do need to mention this - they see what I did when I passed through Medjugorje and was shocked to see the souvenir shops open and this in Medjugorje during Easter. We all live a nice life because of the apparitions but what example do we set? God will grant you His blessing and you will earn three times as much tomorrow. If it were up to me, restaurants would not have meat on their menus on Fridays because we have to show people where we live even in this way; we have to be a role-model for the rest of the world so that people see in us what the Gospa teaches us.

When I visited the late Pope John Paul II, he said: "Look after Medjugorje, Medjugorje brings hope to the entire world." Do we really do this? Do we bring hope to the rest of the world? I really do not wish to criticize or judge anybody, but I want to invite everybody to think within their hearts whether what we are doing is right and whether we are being examples of what our Mother is teaching us.

The late Fr. Slavko dreamt that those moments when the Gospa appears - twenty minutes to seven - are visible and are respected, that everybody close his shop and that people pray in silence.

This would be the true Medjugorje, this would be what pilgrims expect of us. I repeat once again, we all eat the bread that the Gospa provides for us, so let us show everybody that we eat it, let us prove that we are worthy of it. Imagine the beauty of it, that these moments of the apparitions are respected, that Sundays were respected as the day of the Lord and that people, who visit Medjugorje, saw this; wouldn't it be beautiful? Let's pray for this.

These apparitions are unique mainly due to their duration. The visionaries are also on a special mission – you speak of the Gospa's messages on a daily basis, you meet with pilgrims; even though the visionaries have their own families, they have devoted their lives to the Gospa's messages. Do you feel that this is a setback when comparing your lives with the lives of others, the lives of ordinary people, or do you consider it a reward?

With the help of God and prayer, I try to do whatever the Gospa asks of me. I pray for it. I know that I could pray more and that I could be a better person; I know that I could do more for pilgrims. We all can be better. In Medjugorje, we are also responsible for our actions towards pilgrims.

Do you ever think to yourself: *Lord, why did this need to happen to me?*
The thought never crossed my mind; I never asked for this, this is God-given. However, when I feel that my strength is leaving me, I sometimes say: *"My Lord, how could You entrust me with such a task, what was it that You saw in me, do You not see that I cannot do this?"* But then I also say: *"Forgive me, You know that deep in my heart I do not mean what I say."*

Nobody has special privileges before God and the Gospa.
Before God, you and I and everybody else are equal. Nobody has privileges before God and the Gospa. I learned this during the apparitions, especially during the first month of the apparitions when I was in Sarajevo. When I would be brought in for interrogation, I would think to myself: *"When I come back, the Gospa will tell me not to be afraid, that She will be with me".* But nothing of the sort happened. I received my messages just like the visionaries who were in Bijakovići. I was treated the same. I felt sorry for myself, I felt alone and abandoned. A month later, I asked myself why I expected to be treated differently, since for God there are no privileged. If you are having a difficult time, take the rosary in your hands, pray to God, fast, and God will be with you. This is the reason why I think that we are all the same before God. He just has different missions for each

of us. He chose the six of us to spread His messages, but the Gospa needs all of you, She needs apostles. In a message on the second of the month, She said: "Dear children, I invite you, open your hearts to me so that I may enter into them and make you to my apostles." This means that we are all important to God. Those, who think that we, the visionaries, are more important than others, are very wrong. God loves all pilgrims and all people the same. If a mother has five children, she will not love one child more than the other, she loves them all but each of them in a different way. She approaches them all individually but the love remains the same. This is why I do not consider myself as more important. I am the same as all the mothers and women in Medjugorje.

The Gospa does not only ask us to pray, She wants us to lead exemplary lives. When She asks us to pray for those, who have not yet experienced God's love, She asks of us to do things Her way - to feel love for the non-believers, to love them as if they were our brothers and sisters, who were not as lucky as we were to have the opportunity to experience His love. Only when one feels this can one pray for these people; however, we must never criticize or judge them. They need to be loved, we need to pray for them and we need to be examples to them – the way our Mother does, with love and prayer.

Ivanka, Jakov and you received your ten secrets, while Vicka, Ivan and Marija – who still have daily apparitions – have received only nine. During an interview you said that none of the secrets concern you personally, that all the secrets concern the future of the world. Regarding the secrets, what kind of future awaits us?

Secrets are secrets. I will try to explain their meaning as follows: If we follow the Gospa and know that She has been with us for so many years, we must ask the following question: Would the Gospa be with us for so many years if something bad was awaiting us or is She here to help us save ourselves? I always tell pilgrims not to trust those, who try to intimidate us, because faith that comes out of fear is not true faith. Trust those, who talk to you of love, because only faith that comes from love is true faith.

And the secrets...
I say all this also when I talk about the secrets: Do not be afraid! We walk with our Mother. Even on the 18th of last March, She said: *"I extend my hands to you"* – what, therefore, should we be afraid of? After all, why even talk about the secrets anyway? What the Gospa teaches us is to always be ready to come before God, not to concern ourselves with the secrets. What happens will be God's will, our duty is to readily wait for it.

One of the secrets concerns the sign, which the Gospa promised to leave in Medjugorje. Have you seen this sign and do you know when this will occur?
I know when the sign will take place and it will be a gift for us all. It will be clear that this sign is not man-made and that it is from God. This is all I can say.
Where will the sign stand?
On Apparition Hill.

When will the revealing of the secrets take place?
I chose Fr. Petar Ljubičić to divulge the secrets I received. I will reveal to him what and when something will happen ten

days before the events take place. We will pray and fast for seven days. After that, three days before the event takes place, Fr. Petar Ljubičić will reveal the secrets to everyone. He has no choice whether or not to reveal the secrets - he has to reveal them to everyone. This is the will of God and, as he accepted this mission, he needs to fulfill it according to God's will.

However, I always stress, we should not talk about the secrets, we should pray. If we recognize God as our father and the Gospa as our mother, then we should not be afraid of anything.

It is known that the secrets revealed to you are written down on some kind of parchment, a material that does not exist on earth. No other person can read this text?

Yes, this is true. There is no need to hide this parchment because no one but me can read it.

Mirjana, you had the last daily apparition at Christmas 1982. You have written an elaborate report of it. How did you feel when you found out that you would no longer have daily apparitions, that you would no longer see the Gospa every day?

It was the most painful moment of my life. Even when I talk about this today after all these years, I feel like crying. When it happened, I simply couldn't believe it. *How could I live tomorrow? How could I live without the apparitions?* I honestly thought it was impossible and that the Gospa would change Her mind. The next day, during the usual time of the apparitions, I knelt and prayed. The following day, I did the same and this agony went on for a month. After a month had passed, God gave me the strength to understand and accept this as a fact, and so I slowly began to carry on with my life.

I repeat once again, this was the most agonizing pain I have ever experienced in my life. I thought that this was not possible, that I would die, that God could not do this to me.

Since then you have had apparitions on the 18ᵗʰ of March every year. This is what the Gospa had promised you during your last daily apparition. How do you prepare for the apparitions and what does this day mean to you?

Let me first explain something. Many people think that I have apparitions on this day because it is my birthday. However, the apparitions do not occur on this date because of my birthday. The Gospa never congratulated me on my birthday. She does not come because of my birthday.

I always prepare myself for these apparitions with prayer and fasting. The days before March 18ᵗʰ and the days prior to the second of every month are important to me so that I can prepare in peace for the apparition. But God obviously does not wish for me to have this, as it is exactly during these days that the greatest number of pilgrims come and want to talk to me, see me, hear me. It is during these days that I thank God for the night because I cannot be alone in silence and prayer during the day. But I thank God also for this because this is what He wanted for me so that I improve. How long this will go on I do not know.

Since August 2, 1987, on the second of every month, you hear the voice of the Gospa within, but you also see Her for some time since then. This is when you pray with the Gospa for the non-believers or, as the Queen of Peace likes to say, for *those who have not yet experienced the love of God*. Are these apparitions any different from those you have on the 18ᵗʰ of March or are they the same?

For a short period of time there was only a voice within me; soon after, it turned into apparitions on the second of every month. During the last regular apparition, the Gospa had told me that I would also have other apparitions and they started on August 2, 1987. I do not know for how long I will have them. These apparitions differ because they occur in order to pray for those who have not yet experienced the love of God, for the non-believers.

The Gospa has started a great movement through these apparitions on the second of each month and through prayer - prayer for the non-believers has spread throughout the world. Many people testify that this prayer has spread across the world, many pray for others, but also many prayer groups have been formed with this intent. If you take a look at Medjugorje, there are more pilgrims here on the second day of each month than usual and many of them testify that they have changed their lives. They do not testify of physical healing but of the spiritual healing that they experienced here. I think this is most important because man can enter Heaven without an arm and a leg but cannot enter with a sin in his soul. When we pray for those, who have not yet experienced the love of God, we also pray for ourselves, for our children, for our future. Who can say of himself that he is a good believer and that he is following God? On the contrary, I am afraid of those who speak in this fashion. I try to be a good believer. I try to do what God asks of me but only God knows how good a believer I am. Therefore, when we pray for them, we also pray for ourselves.

The Gospa does not ask of us to only pray, She also wants us to be good examples. When She asks us to pray for those, who have not experienced the love of God, She asks us to do it Her way, to first feel love for the non-believers, to love them as brothers and sisters who were not as lucky as we were to experience God's love. When we feel this, then we can pray for them but we must not criticize and judge them. First, we need to love them, pray for them and be examples to them. The way our Mother does - with love and prayer.

Last winter after an apparition, you said that the Gospa was sad, as sad as She had never been during any of Her apparitions. What saddened Her the most?

She is most sad when She sees that we are not going down the right path. She loves us like a mother and everyone is special and important to Her. She takes care of each and everyone of us individually. She is most sad when She sees that Her children choose the path of doom rather than salvation.

It hurts to see Her cry, but it is even more agonizing to see the indescribable pain and sadness in Her face, when Her face winces with pain, when the pain is so strong that I do not need to see Her tears to understand in how much pain She is and how sad She is. I can depict the pain She feels by looking at Her face, and all because of us. She gives us so much and does so much for us and, yet, we don't want to make even the smallest step forward - not for Her but for ourselves; this is terrible. During the apparition that you have mentioned, I felt as if I was going to die, I thought that I would not be able to survive. I was ill for three days after that apparition. Then God gave me the strength not to see Her face constantly before my eyes and not to feel Her pain so strongly. Somehow the faith arose within me that we could wipe away Her tears and lessen Her pain. When I say *we,* I mean all of us, not only the visionaries and the priests. When the Gospa says *"dear children"*, then She speaks to all mankind. All people are Her dear children.

When is the Gospa happiest?
When She talks about Jesus. Then She has the most beautiful smile on Her face. Whenever She shows us Jesus, the love of God, She has the most beautiful indescribable smile. Together with Jesus, She offers us love and hope. After this, I also feel different; it hurts less when the apparition ends.

You have been a visionary for 27 years. Whenever you have an apparition, you see Heaven. The Gospa has on more than one occasion told us that we are living in a time of grace. How should we live, today and also tomorrow? We are witnessing that worldly possessions are becoming more important than spiritual possessions; in wealthy countries less and less people are going to church and, despite our wealth, human hearts are becoming poorer and poorer. How should we live what the Gospa expects of us? How can we resist the temptations of our time and live the messages?
Today's world offers us everything, but only Jesus can offer us peace. You can acquire all earthly possessions, but you will never be content because you will always want more, and more and still more and, yet, it will never be enough. You will never be satisfied because you will not have what is most important - peace. Peace, true peace, can only be attained through Jesus Christ.

Without Jesus, we are destitute and peace is not within us. To those, who wish to hear the testimonies and the messages of the Gospa, I always say: Start with small steps, step by step. Never say: "I will pray the three rosaries, I will fast twice a week…" - you'll get lost, you will give up because you are a weak person. Allow faith to grow within you, allow God to grow within you. The Gospa showed us this through an example. When She first appeared, She asked us to pray seven Our Fathers, Hail Mary's, Glory Bes and The Creed on our knees every day. Only later, She invited us to pray the rosary; to fast every Friday. Even later, She asked us to pray the second rosary, then the third rosary and then to fast on Wednesdays… So She took us a step at a time. I always tell pilgrims to take it slowly – to pray one Our Father today, but to be together with God. This Our Father should truly be an Our Father. Then, tomorrow, add a Hail Mary and, the day after tomorrow, add a Glory Be. Slowly, God will give you the strength and will awaken the wish within you to follow Him and His path one step at a time, as the Gospa has taught us. If one wants something, one can always find the time. Parents show their strength by knowing when it is time to pray. When the time for prayer has come, televisions must be turned off, also computers and everything else and prayers are said. If someone does not want to pray, he will always find a reason why he cannot do so. We can have everything we desire but, if we do not have Jesus, we have nothing. Without Him, we are poor and have no peace.

I would like to ask you a question concerning the life of the youth today. How can we bring the message and the Gospel to them when they are constantly distracted by the glamour of the world?

Here I also stress: Love must always be in the first place. The Gospa says that the responsibility of parents towards their children is immense. We are the ones, who need to sow the seeds of faith in our children. How can we talk of the importance of Holy Mass with them when it is obvious to them that Holy Mass is not the center of our lives? How can we tell them of the importance of prayer if they do not see us pray? Above all, children need to feel the love within their families and then the parents must be good examples to them. Setting an example is very important. If we have sewn the seed of faith in our children, our children will, undoubtedly, follow in our footsteps. It is only a matter of time when this seed will grow to flourish and produce a fruit of faith. Nothing can be gained by criticizing, arguing and yelling, one can only prosper through love, prayer and by setting examples. This is also so with the Gospa, She is a mother who loves us unconditionally.

When children grow up and go off into the world but do not lead a life of faith, what can we do? We need to say: "Mother Mary, I give them to You, I place them into Your hands, I will pray for them and You, please, do the rest." And you can be sure that She will. Not today, not tomorrow, not when you wish for it to happen, but when God thinks the time is right. Never give up, because whoever has faith has hope.

If someone, who knows nothing about the apparitions, were to come to you and ask you to describe the Gospa, Her looks, Her messages, Her desires, that is everything that has been going on in Medjugorje for so many years, how would you explain this to that person? Who is the Gospa, what does She want of us and what does She wish to teach us?

I was asked a similar question by my Muslim classmates in Sarajevo. They asked me who the woman I see was. I told them that the Gospa is a mother, a mother who loves unconditionally, who loves without limits, that everyone is important to Her, that each person is the center of Her life – each and every person is Her child. She is love, She gives love and She asks for love. For me, She is my mother, our Gospa, who comes here to me. She asks of you the same – only love, to just love your neighbor as you love yourself, to see Jesus Christ in every person. When you succeed to see Jesus Christ in every person, then you have fulfilled Her wish, you are walking down God's path, you have experienced the love of God. This is what I say to all, who have never heard of the Gospa and of Her apparitions.

What does one of your prayer days look like?
I get up before everybody so that I can pray the rosary. During the day, I pray the rosary once more because prayer is my conversation with God. Whenever I am tired and can retreat, I pray the rosary and seven Our Fathers. Also, not a day goes by that I don't pray the Rosary of Saint Anthony, this to me is unimaginable, as Saint Anthony is my saint and protector. I was always ashamed to ask the Gospa for something concerning my own life outside the apparitions. I thought that I get so much just by seeing Her face so, through all these years, I have brought my concerns to Saint Anthony. On Tuesdays, I also fast in honor of Saint Anthony, I read the Bible and this is how I talk with God; I like to converse and talk to Him.

I also like to talk to Jesus. For me, the most difficult message of the Gospa is to see Jesus Christ in every person. In some people I simply cannot see Jesus Christ straight away so, when I pray, I say: "Jesus, try to see Yourself in this person." But then, I quickly add: "Forgive me Jesus, You know that I do not mean this at the bottom of my heart." Prayer is my repose, these are moments I jealously treasure.

Many people from all over the world come. What are their wishes?

People seek God. Naturally, some come with wishes that anger me, for example, I get angry when they depict me as somebody important. I cannot smile immediately because it is not me who is important but our Mother and what She does for us. This bothers me. We are all equal before God. If we follow God's path, then one must not think that someone is more important than God. There are no people of more or less importance before God. We are all equal before Him. The Gospa is with us for almost 27 years and not once has She said: "Dear Croats, dear Italians, dear Americans." She always says: "Dear children." Never did She say: "*Dear Mirjana.*" I am just like you, like everybody else, there are no persons, who are more or less important. Do not try to make more of me; I am like you, one of those who is walking this path and trying to do what the Gospa wishes.

What about your family?

I would not be able to do all I do without the help and support of my husband Marko. Thanks to God, I have the support I need in my husband and children. If I am with pilgrims, my husband helps our children with their homework... He also helps me with everything. Together, we try to do what God wishes of us.

As far as our children are concerned, it was important to us that we explain to them from the start, while they were still very young, that their mom is like other women, that I am not special. First, we brought God and faith closer to them, we told them that God does not choose people because they are important or better for some reason but because, in certain moments, He needs certain people and that is why He chose me.

Once, when Marija was two and a half years old – I had never spoken of the apparitions with Her because I thought that she was too little to understand – she was playing with her friend in the living room. I kept an eye on them. At some stage, her friend told her what a good driver her mother was. My Marija responded by saying that that was nothing, that her mother speaks with the Gospa every day. She knew this without me telling her about the apparitions. This is why parents must set an example, why they must pray and love God.

Here is another example: Once, when Veronika was still little, I was talking to a group of Italian pilgrims. When I finished, they hugged and kissed me. Later, Veronika told me that they hadn't understood anything. When I asked her why she thought so, she said that they kissed me but I was not the one, who was important, the Gospa was. This made me happy because I see that they understand that I am not important, that the Gospa is the important one and that we are all equal before Her.

Mirjana, what does the Gospa mean when She says that these are the last apparitions of this kind on earth?

I am glad that you asked me this because people often twist words because they are looking for miracles. What the Gospa said is that this was Her last time on earth in this manner. I never understood those words to mean that She would never appear again, that She would not come again. She wished to say that these are the last apparitions with so many visionaries, for so many years, with so many messages and in such great numbers. I think that this is the essence of Her message. This is the same as when the Gospa said in one of Her messages: "I give you my motherly blessing, from today on, you are that blessing." Some people understood this message to mean that they should bless one another, this left me speechless. Only a priest can bless another person, a priest and no one else. With this message, the Gospa wished to say that our lives should be a blessing to others, that those around us experience God's love, but not that we place our hands on others and bless them. This can only be done by a priest.

On the second of every month during the apparition when the Gospa blesses us and the devotional objects, She says: *"I give you my motherly blessing, however, the greatest blessing you can receive on earth is that of a priest. My Son blesses you through the priest. Do not forget that their hands have been blessed by Jesus."*

You visited Pope John Paul II?

Yes, but only once during a general audience where he blessed me along with all the others. At this occasion, the priest who accompanied me shouted: "This is Mirjana from Medjugorje!" The pope returned, blessed me once more and left. I said to the priest: "You see father, he also thinks that I need to be blessed twice."

Later that afternoon, we received a message to come to Castel Gandolfo the next morning. Meeting Pope John Paul II was an unforgettable experience. The pope said that if he were not the pope, he would already have been in Medjugorje. He did not ask me anything about the secrets, he just asked about the Gospa, about Her beauty and Her love. He asked that the pilgrims pray for his intentions and to preserve Medjugorje, as it is the hope for the whole world.

Jakov Čolo

Jakov Čolo, the youngest of the Medjugorje visionaries, was born on March 6, 1971, in Sarajevo. He had his last daily apparition on September 12, 1998, when he received the tenth secret. During this apparition, the Gospa promised that She would appear to him every year on Christmas Day. Jakov lives in Bijakovici with his wife Analisa and his three children Arijana, David and Mirjam. He prays especially for the ill.

MY CHILDHOOD
WITH THE GOSPA

Ivanka and Mirjana were the first to see the Gospa on June 24, 1981. Later, a few more children saw Her. When and from whom did you first hear of the events that occurred that day?

On June 25th, I was at Marija Pavlović's home. Later that afternoon, Vicka came and told us what had happened the day before on Podbrdo. She told us that they were planning to go to the same place again to see whether the Gospa would come once more. Vicka came back after a while and told us that the Gospa had appeared again and so we went with her. When we arrived at the foot of the mountain, we saw a figure of a woman inviting us with a movement of her hand to come closer - so, we did.

You are a few years younger than the rest of the visionaries. Were you friends, did you all play together?

No, I did not hang out or play with them because I was a few years younger than they. I would sometimes go over to Marija's house; Mirjana is my cousin but she lived in Sarajevo and so we rarely saw each other. Ivan was my direct neighbor but, as he was older than me, he had his own friends. It was simply God's will that I visited Marija that day and that we all went to Podbrdo together.

Describe this first apparition. How did you feel, what did you think, what did you do, how did the Gospa look?

It is difficult to describe those first moments and what I felt. As I said, we saw a female figure motioning to us to come closer. I was afraid, very afraid and I wished to run off, to hide, but I also felt a strong urge to meet this person. I can't remember how we found ourselves up on the hill, but I remember the best part of all – when we first knelt before the Gospa, when I first looked into Her eyes, when we felt and were overcome by Her great love for us. I felt loved and protected. It is difficult, almost impossible to explain, because this can only be felt in one's own heart.

When you came down the hill you said: "Now that I have seen the Gospa, I am not afraid to even die."

These words only confirm what we felt. There are no adequate words, which could better describe the Gospa, Her apparitions and the feelings during the apparitions. The human language is not rich enough to explain all this.

Have you ever had doubts concerning the apparitions, that they could be an illusion, since none of the visionaries had ever heard of the apparitions in Lourdes and Fatima?

There was no doubt in my mind whatsoever because what I had felt could only be from God. I had these feelings from the very beginning and they have never changed to this day.

From the very first days on, there were various accusations – that you were liars, that you made the whole matter up, that you were all hallucinating, that drugs played a role in all this, that you were put up to it by someone...

Were you afraid of such stories, of all the medical examinations, of the interrogations by the militia and also by people from within the Church?

We absolutely felt no fear as God gave us the strength and the Gospa was with us. Sometimes I got angry because they accused a young boy, who was telling the truth, that he was a liar; it is normal that this made me angry. We tried so hard to convince people that we were not liars, that we really see the Gospa. As I grew older, I realized that people cannot be convinced with words to believe, we can only pray for them and that is what we do. Faith in God is something that every person needs to find within his own heart.

From the very beginning, all the visionaries have described the apparitions. Still, can you tell us what an apparition looks like. How do you prepare yourself? How do you know when the Gospa is coming? Describe the apparition itself and how the Gospa leaves.

We always prepare for the apparitions by praying; we pray the rosary. When the Gospa is about to appear, we see a flash of light three times and everything around us disappears and all we see is the Gospa. It is difficult to describe the apparition itself. Actually, it is impossible because the peace and joy one feels during the apparition is indescribable. It is difficult to describe in human language. It can only be experienced. We always pray an Our Father and a Glory Be with Our Lady, we pray for all the pilgrims and those who have come to Medjugorje, and we also pray for the ill.

During the apparitions, do all the visionaries hear the same words or does the Gospa speak to each of the visionaries separately?

There were apparitions during which the Gospa would talk to all of us together and there were also apparitions during which the Gospa would talk to us separately, when each of us only heard something important for ourselves. I have been to apparitions with Marija during which the Gospa gives Her the monthly message, but I could never hear them.

Describe what the Gospa looks like, Her age, Her face, Her hair, Her clothes...

I always see the Gospa as a young woman. She wears a grey dress and a short white veil; She has blue eyes and black hair, and She always stands on top of a cloud. This is what can be described with words, but it is impossible to describe Her beauty. We have had artists of all kinds, who wished to paint the Gospa or make a statue of Her. They have tried everything but it can never be done, however great the artist may be. The beauty of the Gospa is what you feel in your heart during the apparition. When we were young, we asked the Gospa how it was possible that She is so beautiful. This is what She said: "Because I love. If you want to be beautiful, you must love."

How did your peers react, especially when you attended school in September, considering that you had become known throughout the world by this time? You were sought out by journalists, priests, believers and by people who were curious to find out what it was all about.

We all grew up together, we were all Christians and Catholics and, therefore, I had no problems with friends and other children. They took what I said seriously.

Many people, who are ill and have different problems, have asked Our Lady for help and their recovery. How does the Gospa answer such prayers?

The Gospa has always answered every request with: "Pray and have strong faith." This is true for all pilgrims, who come to Medjugorje, and we know that many of them are ill. I always say: "First of all, let us pray for the healing of our hearts." Today, it is our hearts that are most ill. In order to accept our illness and not think of it as a punishment from God but rather as God's plan, we first need to heal in our hearts, we need to pray and have strong faith.

From all your meetings with the Gospa, did you understand why apparitions are necessary since we have the Bible, the Sacraments and holy Mass?

During all these years, I have realized that the Gospa is a mother, who loves Her children, and that, like any mother on earth, She is concerned about Her children. The Gospa came here to wake us up so that we may start living. To live means to live with God. The rest, life without God, is not a life.

The visionaries have passed on the words of the Gospa as these being Her last apparitions in this manner. Some have interpreted this in various ways, some even speak of catastrophes. How did you interpret Her words?

I interpreted it this way: These are the last apparitions that will last for so long, with so many messages and visionaries, but not that the Gospa will not appear anymore.

During the first days, months and years, various people have maintained that they have seen miraculous signs on Cross Mountain, Apparition Hill and at the church.

Many have also said that they have experienced various blessings and have even been healed. Have you ever talked about this with the Gospa?

We have always prayed for sick and those who have asked us to do so. I have never asked the Gospa whether any of these people have actually been cured or not. This is God's plan and when I speak with pilgrims I tell them that they should not come to Medjugorje for the signs because the greatest sign that one can experience in Medjugorje is to change oneself; this means to start to live with God. For me, this is the greatest miracle; however, if anyone experiences a miracle, thank God.

You have had your last daily apparition on September 12, 1998. How did you feel when the Gospa told you the day before that this would be your last apparition?

The Gospa did not tell me during the apparition on September 11th that this was to be my last apparition, She told me that I would receive the tenth secret. Mirjana and Ivanka had already received their tenth secret and that apparition was their last daily apparition; however, I hoped that it would be different for me, there is always a glimmer of hope. It is hard to describe the pain I felt when the Gospa told me that She would not be coming to me every day anymore. I asked myself millions of questions: Why? How will it be possible not to see the Gospa anymore? What will I do during the time of the apparition? How will I be able to bear not to see the Gospa, who had been appearing to me daily for 17 years? I can say that I have grown up with the Gospa, She had taken me by my hand and had guided me through my life... However, the Gospa had told us: "Pray and you will receive all the answers to your questions!" That is what I did – I prayed and the Gospa gave me the strength to be able to accept everything. I am grateful to God for everything that He has given me, for the time in which He has sent me the Gospa and for seeing Her with my own eyes. But I also realized that it may not be that important to see Her with your eyes, but with the eyes of your heart. She is still there today. The Gospa is always with me, also when I don't see her with my own eyes, but with the eyes of my heart.

The day after your last apparition you had a prayer program scheduled to take place in Haiti. Were you in doubt as to whether you should go or not?
After the last apparition, I wanted to block out everything, I didn't feel like going to that prayer meeting. I constantly thought about why I should go since I no longer saw the Gospa every day. I felt an agonizing pain in my heart. However, it was difficult to tell the people, who had planned this event for over a year, that I would not be going. I prayed and asked the Gospa for help, I left everything in God's hands and went to the prayer meeting. This is one of the poorest places on earth, but between 70.000 to 80.000 people turned up. Seeing such joy and such a yearning for God – people were praying and singing, even though some of them may have had nothing to eat that day – I realized that prayer was their food, I realized that many were wealthier than we, even though they were poor. They were wealthy because they had God. I recognized the Gospa in every person that was at the prayer meeting, I saw the Gospa was there, even though I couldn't see Her, She was there with me.

How did you get through the next days, they must have seemed completely empty to you?
Through prayer and only prayer.

Your annual apparition takes place on Christmas Day each year so, on that day, you have a double blessing: Christmas and the apparition. How do you prepare for this day?

The whole year is a preparation for this day, I prepare through prayer, with my family and my children, through personal prayer and fasting. The Gospa gave me a great gift – an apparition at Christmas. Christmas for me is always an indescribably joyous occasion, it is a gift for which I am always grateful to God.

The Gospa has taken you and Vicka to Heaven, hell and Purgatory. Can you describe this event?

I was eleven years old then. That day, the apparition did not take place at the usual time. We were frightened because the apparition did not take place during the regular time, for which we prepare with prayer. On that day, the Gospa came suddenly and we were frightened. We were even more scared when She told us that we were to go with Her. I thought I was going to die, I didn't want to go because I had never thought of death before. When the Gospa told us this, I told Her to take Vicka because she was one of eight children in her family and I was the only child in mine. But the Gospa said: *"Do not be afraid, I am with you."* Our journey did not last long. The first place that the Gospa showed us was a place of never-ending space in which there was a beautiful light, a light I had never seen on earth. The light could be described as warm and we also saw many people praying in this place. This is how Heaven can be described best because Heaven cannot be described by anybody. What impressed me most about this place was the peace and joy that could be felt, the peace and the joy that could be seen on the faces of these people. It took me a long time to understand what Heaven was and I understood this through prayer. Heaven is not what we see, Heaven is in all of us, in our hearts, and I am sure that each and every one of us can experience Heaven here on earth. If we accept God and put Him on the first place, then we already have Heaven. All pilgrims ask me about this, about experiencing Heaven. I usually answer their questions with a question: "Are we ready for Heaven at every moment? At this precise moment, am I ready to stand before God?" These are the most important questions.

After this, the Gospa showed us a place where there was only darkness. We did not see people here, but we heard groaning and felt convulsions. The Gospa said: *"Pray for the souls in Purgatory, they need your prayers."*

At the end, the Gospa showed us a third place, about which I have never talked nor do I wish to talk about it. It was horrifying.

Did this ever happen again?
No, this was the first and only time.

Mirjana, Ivanka and you have been entrusted with ten secrets, while Vicka, Marija and Ivan, who still have daily apparitions, have received nine secrets. We know how Mirjana will reveal her secrets. Do you know how you will reveal yours?
I have received ten secrets from the Gospa. How they will be revealed I do not know yet. The Gospa has not spoken of this yet.

The Gospa has spoken of Her life with some visionaries. Did She share Her life with you?
No, She has never spoken of Her life with me.

Mirjana has all ten secrets written down on a piece of parchment. How do you keep your secrets? What are they written on?

My secrets are not written anywhere. I have them memorized.

As the secrets are secrets, you cannot talk about them. However, all the visionaries have confirmed that the third secret is the same for all - the sign on Apparition Hill. Did you see the sign and do you know when it will take place?

Yes, I do know when it will take place and, yes, I have seen the sign.

Do the secrets concern your private life or do they concern all of us?

I am not allowed to talk about that.

Is it difficult to keep these secrets? Are you ever tempted to talk about them in detail?

No, this has never happened and I tell the pilgrims not to think of them but to pray instead. As I have already mentioned, our greatest secret is to be ready to step before God at every moment. Every person, who knows God and who lives with God, does not need to be afraid of anything. As soon as the secrets are mentioned, catastrophes and wars come to mind. It is better to think of positive things, to think of one's own life because, if we have God in our life, we do not need to fear anything.

From a ten-year-old boy, who has had daily apparitions and has had to convey the messages from Heaven, you are now a grown man and father. As a father, you have worries and responsibilities; did you ever think to yourself: *Dear God, why did you give me such a burden?*

I will never be able to show God how grateful I am to Him for the gift He has given me to see the Gospa. This is a great gift to me, my family and the world. Still, it is difficult sometimes, we are all human. We all know how many pilgrims come to Medjugorje and many of them, I meet. This is sometimes also difficult, but, thank God, we can carry on.

How do you realize within your own family what the Gospa has been teaching us for the last 27 years?
We live this with prayer, fasting and by raising our children. I always tell everybody that we are a family just like any other, a family that wishes to live the messages of the Gospa, to raise our children in the faith so that they may be true Christians – not because they are children of visionaries but as children in a Christian family. We pray and fast with our children, we talk with them and we convey God's love onto them...

Every visionary has a special gift, a special intention. What is yours?
Vicka and I pray especially for the sick, especially for the healing of hearts. I always tell pilgrims that it is not wrong to pray for physical health, for healing, but we always need to add: *"God, may Your will be done."* Most of the time, we think of God and reach out for Him only when we are in trouble and in need, when we are ill and overwhelmed with problems. But God should always be in our heart, at every moment, because God is our strength and He is the answer to everything we are looking for in life.

When we look with open and honest hearts at our parish and many other parishes in the world, we see that many have experienced change. The fruits of the appari-

tions are undeniable, they are evident in the conversions, the many confessions and the number of pilgrims who come. Prayer groups have been inspired by the Queen of Peace and many live according to the messages. Still, many have problems to accept the apparitions. Today, after so many years, do statements, claiming that these are not the fruits of the Holy Spirit, that everything is made up and is the result of hallucination, hurt you?

Of course, rejection and other negative statements hurt me. I mean, I saw the Gospa with my own eyes, better, yet, I have experienced Her in my heart. When I was a child, I would get angry at such statements, but now not anymore, now I pray for these people. What is happening in Medjugorje is God's plan and God will continue with it, there is nothing anybody can do about it.

Why do people have such cold hearts and do not see these fruits? Is it not enough to see so many people at the church in Medjugorje, so many waiting in line for confession, many in wheelchairs, so many priests at the altar, thousands of faithful at Holy Mass, tens of thousands of young people from all over the world who come here to pray in the hot sun instead of going to the beaches, so many people praying on Apparition Hill and on Cross Mountain, and the many priests who felt their calling precisely here in Medjugorje?

This question should be asked of these people; I often ask myself why people have such cold hearts. The Gospa has been with us for 27 years, She calls us Her *"dear children"* and She always thanks us at the end of each apparition. She thanks us; instead, we should thank God and the Gospa for Her presence here... We must pray for these people, because She has said that even wars can be stopped through prayer and fasting. I am sure that these people can experience change with the help of our prayers.

Finally, what message do you have for people today, a message coming from a person, who experienced daily encounters with Heaven and who has once been taken to Heaven?

I can only repeat the words of the Gospa from the very beginning of the apparitions: *"Dear children, open your hearts and leave the rest unto me!"* Let us put our lives into the hands of God and the Gospa, and we will understand what life truly is.

THE MOST UNIQUE
SIGN OF MEDJUGORJE
IS CONVERSION

I was ten years old when the apparitions of Our Lady began. Before this event, I lived like every other child in the village, I played with my peers and friends, I was raised in a Christian family, my parents taught me that God exists, that the Gospa exists. I prayed and lived faith as any ten-year-old child.

It Is Difficult to Explain How Loved and Protected I Felt
On June 25, 1981, when I first saw the Gospa, when I first looked into Her eyes and felt the love She had for me, for all of us, it is difficult to describe how loved and protected I felt. At that moment, all talk ceases, only our hearts speak and my heart said: "May this moment never end." I received a great gift from God, the gift to see the Gospa. But, at the same time, I received another even greater gift – through the Gospa I met Jesus.

When the Gospa invited us to live Her messages, when She called for prayer, conversion, peace, fasting, Holy Mass – as a child I asked myself, how to accept all this. In my heart I understood the words the Gospa said to us: *"Dear children, it is enough that you open yourselves to me, the rest I will take care of myself."* In Medjugorje, we always need to invite people to open their hearts to the Gospa, to put our lives into Her hands. If we don't have God, we don't have life; but if we have God, we have everything.

We often think that, if we have material riches, we have everything and we forget all about God. On the contrary, without God, we are poor; only those, who have God in their hearts, are whole and wealthy.

My Life Began When I Felt Jesus and Mary in My Heart
My true life began when I was ten years old, at that precise moment, when I truly experienced Jesus and the Gospa, when I felt them in my heart.

The Gospa invited us to pray. She said: *"Dear children, pray with your hearts, feel the joy, the peace and the peace that prayer brings. May prayer become your joy, because you cannot pray if you think that you must pray."* The heart needs to feel the need to pray, then prayer will become joy.

When the Gospa told us this, I asked myself as a child how it was possible to pray with the heart, how this should happen. I realized that prayer with the heart was a gift from God, a gift that God wishes to give everybody. I said to God and to the Gospa: "Dear God, dear Gospa, from now on I wish to pray with my heart, I wish to feel prayer in my heart, I wish to feel the joy of prayer, I wish to feel peace in prayer." Then I began to pray and, slowly, I felt the joy of prayer. I searched for a place where I could pray and I didn't find it difficult to pray anymore. We all need to ask the Gospa to help us pray with our hearts so that we may feel the beauty of prayer.

To Be Holy Means to Have God in Our Hearts
So many times the Gospa has called us to start to pray in our families. Nothing can bring a family together like prayer. The Gospa says: *"Place God on the first place in your families, make time for God."* In another message the Gospa

said: *"I wish that every family becomes holy."* I wondered what it meant *to be holy.* To be holy means to have God in our hearts, to live with God. To be holy also means to have peace in your family, to be able to talk to your parents, to be able to help others, to smile at other people, to extend your hand to your neighbor and to love all people.

The Gospa also says: *"Dear children, fast."* I know that many, who come to Medjugorje, have problems with fasting, while many wonder why to fast at all. Remember how many times the Gospa has repeated here in Medjugorje: *"Dear children, with prayer and fasting, you can even stop wars."*

We only think of God when we are suffering or have crosses to bear. Only then do we ask: "God, where are You, have You forgotten me, why don't You help me?" Instead of asking this, we should ask ourselves where we were, how much time we spent with God and if we put God in the first place. God is always close to us but through our omissions and sins we don't want Him near us.

The Gospa says: *"Dear children, convert, convert your hearts!"* One does not come to Medjugorje to see the visionaries or to seek visible signs. The greatest sign in Medjugorje is conversion, a new life with God. This new life should be brought into our families and we should be witnesses to change in our families. We need to show within our families how beautiful it is to live with God. Unfortunately, many are afraid to convert. But when we experience God and God's love, then we realize that we have everything.

It Is Not Possible to Deny the Love of the Gospa

During the first days of the apparitions, we were asked to deny everything, we were even asked to say that we didn't see the Gospa. We responded that this was impossible to deny, especially the fact that we had seen the Gospa and that we had felt Her love in our hearts. It is impossible to deny the Gospa's love. People are the way they are, because we try to do everything on our own, through our own efforts instead of giving our hearts to God and saying: "God, here I am, I give You my heart, my life, and, from now on, You guide my life."

In Medjugorje, the Gospa invites us to pray for peace, above all, to pray for peace in our hearts. If we do not have peace in our hearts, we cannot become close to God and, if we are not close to God, then we cannot accept what the Gospa asks of us.

Every pilgrim should ponder over this message of the Gospa: *"Dear children, if you knew how much I love you, you would cry of joy."* So let us also start to love the Gospa, to love God. Let us truly start to accept God as our Father and the Gospa as our Mother.

A true pilgrimage to Medjugorje should continue when one returns home. Only then will become visible what one has received in Medjugorje and what fruits one has brought home from the pilgrimage.

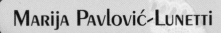
Marija Pavlović-Lunetti

Marija Pavlović-Lunetti was born on the April 1, 1965, in Bijakovići. She has had daily apparitions since June 25, 1981. Since March 1, 1984, Our Lady has given her messages to convey to the parish on every Thursday. Since 1987, Our Lady is giving her messages for the whole world on the 25th of every the month. Nine secrets have been revealed to Marija. For most of the year, Marija lives with her husband Paolo and their children in Monza, Italy.

THE APPARITIONS OF THE GOSPA ARE ALWAYS AN INVITATION TO CONVERT

Marija, how does it feel to be a person, who conveys messages of the Gospa?

Undoubtedly, this is a great joy but also it brings humbleness that one can serve the Gospa. This gift is a daily sign to me that I am a drop in the sea through which God and the Gospa act. In my heart, I always feel a great need to testify, to testify even more, not to get tired and to inspire those, who have chosen holiness.

Did you ever ask the Gospa why She chose you and why this place?

At the beginning, we asked the Gospa this question at least a thousand times. Even among ourselves, we wondered *why us, why not someone else*? I ask myself this question even now when I think about everything, as I am not worthier than others. I have not earned this great gift, this grace bestowed on me by the Gospa. On the other hand, I thank our Creator and the Gospa every day for having chosen me to be a witness to Her love and Her presence here on earth for such a long time.

Decades have passed since the Gospa has first appeared on Podbrdo in Medjugorje. Looking back, describe how you felt those first days, how was your first encounter with the Gospa?

Certainly, one cannot forget that first love, those first encounters. But every day, every encounter with the Gospa is special; every encounter with the Gospa is so overwhelming, it is the most meaningful thing that can happen to me during the day. However, those first encounters with the Gospa are still so fresh in my memory as if they were happening at present. It came as a shock, as a surprise, I felt scared... I had mixed emotions of love, joy, of having been chosen...

Describe one of your apparitions. How do you prepare for it?

For the encounter with the Queen of Peace, I prepare myself by praying - this is most important. Prayer opens us not only towards others but, even more so, towards God.

What does the Gospa look like, can you describe Her beauty?

It is hard to describe the Gospa's beauty with human language. For example, whenever I want to buy a statue or a painting of the Gospa, I search through all of Medjugorje and, in the end, I buy the first statue or painting of Her I had come upon. I simply cannot find anything remotely resembling Her. But one needs to look through the eyes of the people, who have never seen the Gospa. Her smile, Her peace and Her beauty are not to be described. Many times, I have truly tried to describe the appearance of the Gospa but each time I realize that this is impossible.

Please describe the apparition you have on the day of the anniversary of the apparitions. Does this apparition differ from the rest of your apparitions?

It is different in the sense that it is a thanksgiving to God for all that He has given us. But every encounter with the Gospa is a grace. We need to be aware of that and we need to live accordingly.

What does God ask of us through Our Lady? Why are the apparitions going on for so long?

I would say: As long as the Gospa is with us, we are safe. The Gospa's apparitions are always a calling for conversion. The Gospa commits Herself in thousands of ways. Her presence among us is a great grace, She gives us the opportunity to be better. She has shown us, the visionaries, Heaven, hell and also Purgatory, and She told us that She wanted to take us to Heaven with Her - not only us visionaries, but also all those, who have come in contact with Medjugorje. I remember, when we asked the Gospa for how long She would stay with us, She responded with a question: *"Are you tired of me already?"* With this, She meant to say that She was not yet tired of being here with us and that She was expecting more from us. It is Her wish that we do not get tired, not of praying, not of fasting, not of our crosses... The Gospa invites to begin living Heaven here on earth. This has been her most ardent wish throughout all the years of Her apparitions.

On the 25th of every month, the Gospa gives us a message. What is the essence of Her message?

The main essence of Her message is holiness. She continuously invites us to holiness, and the source of holiness is love. Without Her love and Her encouragement, we are nothing. Each of us needs to understand and to accept that the callings of the Gospa are pure love. Her messages are clear. She gives messages through words, but the spirit, the form, the smile is what gives strength; but this cannot be conveyed. I have cried many times, as I felt weak and unable to convey the power and strength of Her words. On the day when Our Lady gives the message for the world, I always try to prepare myself better for this encounter by praying and fasting.

Besides testifying of your experience in other countries, you regularly testify to pilgrims in Italy where you live with your family. Can you tell us about some of your experiences with pilgrims?

The fruits of Medjugorje are truly great. Many prayer groups and communities have been formed, people have converted, changes have occurred within families. For instance, I was invited to an Italian parish where I was welcomed so beautifully, as I had not been welcomed in a long time. The whole parish was involved in the preparations, everything was impeccably organized. There was a sign saying *Welcome Marija* on the entrance of the church. Later, the parish priest told me that sign meant *Welcome Gospa,* and this had been the fruit of a 24-hour- long adoration of the entire parish community.

You have a husband and four children. How do you live holiness and the Gospa's messages within your family?

This is the most difficult part. I think that humbleness and mutual respect is most important in a family. When we feel that we have sinned in this respect, it is important to ask for forgiveness. There should be understanding for one another; this is the only way we can achieve harmony and peace. The Gospa often speaks to us about this.

Your prayer intention is to pray for those, who have devoted their lives to God, and also to pray for the souls in Purgatory?

That's right. I feel a great need to pray for the souls in Purgatory; for those who did not achieve everything necessary to be with God in eternity. Especially since we are attached to the worldly and material things every day, the Gospa cautions us that we realize that our lives on earth are transient, that we are headed to eternity. She also tells us that She wants us to be happy both on earth and in Heaven. This means to discover God and put Him in the first place.

For more than 27 years you have been giving testimony about the apparitions of Our Lady and you have been conveying Her messages to us. You are constantly being asked to speak about your experiences. Don't you get tired of these many encounters?

They do not tire me and also not the other visionaries, even if one would think that so many encounters and testimonies may be tiresome. If one has experienced an encounter with the Gospa and has felt Her love, then serving Her will not tire...

How do you see this parish today? Is it developing in the right direction?

Although I live in Italy for most of the year, I still feel Medjugorje as being my home, it is my home. To this, I can only say that it is alright to build houses and to work, but it is not alright when prayer is being forgotten. Everything that does not bring us closer to God, everything that moves us away from God, is not alright. I always emphasize humbleness; we need to be grateful for all the graces God has given us through Mary in Medjugorje. We need to realize that we are all on the way to holiness, towards which the Gospa leads here through Her presence; She wishes each one of us to attain holiness. That is why we should decide to live a life with God.

OUR LADY'S SCHOOL OF PRAYER

The first prayer that we, the visionaries, and later the whole parish prayed together with Our Lady was seven Our Fathers, Hail Marys, Glory Bes and the Creed. We joyously continued with these prayers each evening after Holy Mass, kneeling down and giving thanks for Her presence among us.

The Rosary

One step at a time, the Gospa invited and encouraged us to pray the rosary - Her favorite prayer. With great joy, we started to pray the Joyful, Sorrowful and Glorious Mysteries. Later, the Gospa encouraged us to pray the fourth mysteries, the Luminous Mysteries that Pope John Paul II gave us. By praying the rosary, we were to ponder upon and live the life of Jesus. Not much time had passed and the Gospa asked us to pray the rosary every day.

The Bible, the Cross and Blessed Objects

She encouraged us to place the Bible in our homes, somewhere where it would be visible and to read it. I remember when She asked us to do so, all of us visionaries went out and bought a Bible and started to read it. Wherever we would go – Apparition Hill, Cross Mountain – we would bring the Bible along. We read it gladly and by reading the Psalms, through prayer, we expressed joy to God.

The Gospa also asked us to put a cross in our homes where it would be visible. She told us to always have blessed objects on us as a sign that we belong to Her. With medals, rosaries and crosses we began to attest that we are Christians, that we belong to the Gospa and that God comes first in our lives.

We Fell in Love with Jesus Through Mary
The Gospa also invited and encouraged us to establish prayer groups within our families and parishes. By doing so, we grew with the Gospa in our religious life, She guides us. After some time, the Gospa invited us to pray for three hours each day. When She asked this of us, we told Her that this was a bit too much to ask of us, that we were not capable of praying this much. She smiled and said: *"When a dear friend comes to visit you, you do not look at the clock and wonder how long your friend will be staying, how much time you will spend with him. Allow Jesus to become your best friend."*

From this moment on, we began a more intense life with Jesus, we fell in love with Jesus through Mary. We followed the messages of Our Lady and started to live what God had asked of us through Mary.

Adoration of the Blessed Sacrament of the Altar
We complied with the messages of Our Lady and started to testify with our lives. The Gospa asked us to adore Jesus in the Blessed Sacrament of the Altar, which we started to do regularly. We first started to do so as a prayer group, we gave thanks to God for what He was doing for us through Mary. We also gave thanks to God for what He was doing through all who were coming and converting here.

The Gospa Does Not Get Tired

During every apparition, I pray to the Gospa for all people, especially for the young and for all who come to Medjugorje, that they may be saved, that they decide for holiness like St. Francis did by attesting to the Risen Christ in a special way. We often see many young people, who are spiritually dead, because they have decided for God knows what evil things.

The Gospa always encourages us to testify and to be aware that Jesus died on the cross for us, and that we attest to the Risen Christ.

Even though the apparitions have been going on for so many years, the Gospa never gets tired. She wants us to be Her outstretched hands and be carriers of Her messages. Therefore, She says: *"Dear children, I intercede for you before my Son, start to convert."*

Even today, the Gospa says: *"Dear children, I am your mother, I love you."*

Let us make good use of this time of grace. The Gospa regularly encourages us to decide for eternal life, to decide for God. This is what Her Son Jesus seeks through Her.

Ivan Dragićević

Ivan Dragićević was born on May 25, 1965, in Bijakovići. He has had daily apparitions since June 24, 1981. Along with his wife Laureen and their children Kristina, Mikaela, Daniel and Matthew, he lives in Boston for part of the year and in Bijakovići for the other. He has been entrusted with nine secrets. His special intention is to pray for the youth.

GOSPA LOVES US AND INVITES US TO BE BRIGHT LIGHTS IN OUR TIRED WORLD

The Queen of Peace has been appearing in Medjugorje for thirty years. If we take into consideration the number of visionaries, the number of years and days, we can see that the apparitions have taken place many times. Ivan, looking back to the beginning, at 1981, did you ever think that this would last for so long?

Honestly, I never thought about that. The apparitions, for me and my life came as a surprise; it was a shock. As a child, then a sixteen-year-old, I never even knew that Gospa could appear. I was a very shy and introverted child and ever so attached to my parents. I did not have many friends and I liked being on my own at school, it was the way I was. Back then I wasn't an eager reader and up till then I had never heard of Lourdes, Fatima and about the apparitions. I had never read anything about it nor did I have any idea that it was possible that Gospa could appear. My parents never spoke about this and whenever we had Bible Education the priest never spoke about the apparitions which took place in the world. Obviously, when the apparition took place, it came as a shock to me. Later, we were told that the apparitions in Lourdes lasted for eighteen days and that, in Fatima, they lasted for a few months. For this reason I thought that the apparitions we experienced would not last much longer. I vividly remember those first days, Apparition Hill, when the people and the villagers who were with us told us to ask Gospa for how long She would be appearing. We did what we were told and we asked Her. I don't know whether She was serious or whether She was joking, but She said, "Have you grown tired of me already?" Never did I dream that this grace would last for so long.

When you look back on the years of grace, tell us what you consider to be most important for yourself, the parish, the believers, the Church and, finally, the world?
The fruits are truly numerous. Gospa is sowing a good seed here. Is this seed falling on fertile ground? Have we prepared this ground? Have we pulled the weeds out so that the seeds can grow into good fruit? When I say this I mean us, our parish, which Gospa has specially chosen to send a message to the world. Our parish has a great, great gift and a grave responsibility towards the world. I don't know whether the parish is aware of this or if some parishioners are aware that the apparitions are still taking place. Talking about the fruits – priesthood and spiritual or physical healing (without spiritual healing there is no physical healing) in my opinion, this is the nucleus – when mankind heals, when people become signs, bright lights within their families and parishes and when they organize prayer groups and adorations. Is it possible to have greater fruits than the ones I have just mentioned? Personally, for me, the biggest sign of the apparitions is the spiritual renewal of the world and humanity, everything else accompanies this. For example, when you see the youth during their prayer meetings, when you see their fervor, prayer, songs, their shiny eyes staring towards the sky, we see that they are ambassadors of peace in the world; they are the ones that carry Gospa's message of peace to the rest of the world. They are the apostles

of this message. Only those who live the message can be apostles. All of us, not only the young, are invited and sent by Gospa to become apostles. Gospa loves us and invites us to become bright lights in our tired world. Let us not be deceived. Gospa also tells us to forget about presidents of countries and governments, She says that only God can give us peace. God has given the power to promote peace to all presidents of the world, to all governments, congresses, senates and parliaments. He gave them the power to work in the name of peace, for man and mankind. Every government that is without God is a government without order and therefore does not accept God's principles and cannot offer peace. We will soon be disappointed in the peace this world offers us. People see true peace in Gospa's messages. If you follow the news in the various media you will notice that we are bombarded with news of wars, riots, floods, divorces and abortions on a daily basis. Man then asks himself *God, how is this possible today, has man become so rigid, so evil; has man truly become so empty and does not recognize the difference between good and bad?* This is why I think that the apparitions, which have lasted for so long, is a turning point for humanity, a turning point for each and everyone of us to become better and to choose good over evil, to abandon sin and to accept the values that God gives us. If we carry on living as we do we will not come far, we shall sink deeper into darkness, into satisfaction with own ourselves. We shall keep withering. This is why I say that we need to accept this path of hope Gospa calls us upon. Gospa leads us onto this path of hope.

If a person who just heard of the apparitions of the Queen of Peace spoke with you now, what would you tell him/her about it?

We have many such encounters and experiences. People who know nothing of the apparitions come to me daily – people who are neither believers nor Catholic. When I meet with such people, I first want to befriend them, then I want to see what they think, what their faith is like, what their desires are. Later on, I gradually tell them about what is happening here: I tell them about the messages and the invitation our Mother has sent us. If this person is of another faith or is not a follower of any religion at all then I cannot talk about Gospa's messages directly because he or she is not familiar with the Gospel. I approach them differently; I tell them about the Gospel, about Christ and Christ's Mother for they cannot otherwise comprehend the message. I have to say that I am very pleased when people leave and go home changed after this because they have found what they had been looking for. The power of the Holy Ghost comes down upon them and there is nothing more satisfying than to see the smile return to their faces. Such people carry many burdens: problems within their families and in their daily lives. When I talk with them I can tell that they are ready to convert and to integrate the experience of grace into their families. These are great values. However, we cannot and may not force someone into doing something, in this case, into believing, which is a great gift. For our own sakes, we need to open up to faith and peace. We often force things and this can be counterproductive, therefore we should not coerce. Whenever a pilgrim comes here, be they a believer or unbeliever, Catholic or other, they should be gently approached with love, be accepted and not ostracized. Through unconditional acceptance we fulfill the first ideal of what Gospa seeks from us: *Dear children, no one must be cast away. All people are equally important and valuable to me. There is no difference between rich and poor.*

I care not for the color of your skin. We are all equally important in Gospa's project, the reason for which She has been coming here for so long.

You yourself have stated that you were introverted and shy as a child and a young boy. Now, you give testament to the messages throughout the world and stand before thousands of people. How did this change in you occur?
I was shy by nature, only open towards my parents and brothers. Believe me, up to 1988, I never stood and spoke before pilgrims. As a boy, I hid under my bed when pilgrims started to visit my house. I used to tell my mother that I didn't want to go outside before them. I served the army during 1986/1987 and a year later I received a Yugoslav passport for the first time ever because I was not allowed one earlier. I visited America for the very first time. I went to Chicago to see my uncle after twenty-six years. Many people in Chicago had heard of Medjugorje. Numerous prayer groups and peace centers were founded. It was there that I opened up and started testifying before crowds. I spoke to people during Masses and at prayer conferences – this was how I started. I started attending prayer meetings throughout the world and spoke before thousands of believers during each of them. Gospa gave me courage. She told me to open up more and to give more when I speak before people who have difficulties, who are wounded and ill. These people were in need of consolation. She led me as She led all six of the visionaries. She told me to encourage people and to give more unto them. This is how I started to openly give testimony.

You mentioned that you served your compulsory military service in Ljubljana, Slovenia. Did you ever feel as if you were under any pressure while you were there?

It was a shock and surprise in a positive sense. I arrived at the army barracks in Šentvid, close to Ljubljana, at the end of June. I hadn't travelled much up till then. I saw Mostar for the very first time when I was taken there for interrogation. At first, I was supposed serve the army in Kragujevac, Serbia but, thanks to the wonderful people at the military department in Čitluk, I was sent to Slovenia – which was more tolerant at the time. The people in the Čitluk army department felt that I would be under less pressure there. Upon arrival I had my haircut and was handed a uniform – the usual army procedure. I didn't have any problems and I felt no stress – maybe the soldiers that were with me there didn't know much about me but my superiors did and, despite that, there were no provocations. I did have a few conversations with my seniors at the army headquarter but nothing that made me feel uncomfortable. I went through a three-month training course and Lieutenant Josip Jeličić from Muća, near Split, appointed me his clerk. I spent the rest of my army service as a clerk and was allowed to go into town everyday if I wanted to. During the afternoons, I would be alone at the office and I had my apparitions there. Before I left home to go to the army, Gospa prepared me and told me that I would not have apparitions during the first few days of the beginning of my service. During this time, I didn't have apparitions but I did hear Her voice in my heart.

Did your lieutenant ever talk with you about the apparitions?

No, even though the other superiors and he knew that I had daily apparitions, we never talked about them. During this time I grew spiritually and, interestingly enough, I was the first soldier who was granted a fifteen day leave to go home, around Christmas time. I couldn't believe I was going home for Christmas!

After coming back from my leave, I needed to report back to the superiors. I was interrogated by a senior in charge of army- base security. He asked me why I went to church while I was on leave. I didn't feel threatened by the situation at all, actually it was quite funny. He just had to do what he was ordered to.

You mentioned that you did not have apparitions during the first days of your army service.
No, I didn't. Gospa prepared me for this. She said that She would be with me and that I would be able to hear Her within my heart. I had my first apparition ten days after arriving at the army.

As you stated earlier and in an interview two years ago, you mentioned that you never heard about the apparitions that took place in Lourdes and Fatima until you had yours on the 24th of June 1981. Did you ever ask yourself why Gospa chose the six of you and Medjugorje?
I ask myself this question many times every single day. I wonder *why me?* There must have been many more young people who prayed more than I did. I'm not saying that I did not pray. I remember, during summer and after lining the tobacco leaves, we would sit in the shade of a wall and we would pray the prayers our mothers taught us. Instead of resting, our three families would get together and pray – my family, Markan Dragićević's family and the family of Jakov's mother, Jaka. Everyday I ask myself *Mother, why me? Now, that You have chosen me, are you pleased with what I do?* Before an apparition I had on my own with Gospa, I was feeling heavy-hearted and this question was constantly on my mind. I decided I'd ask Gospa why She chose me; I wanted to know. During my apparition, I asked Her, "Mother, why me? Why did You choose me?" She smiled in Her

own sweet way and said, "Dear child, you know, I never pick the best." I never asked Her this question again. I, personally, never asked Her why She chose this place but I know the other visionaries did and, to the best of my knowledge, She said that She chose this parish because its people went through a great ordeal in the name of faith and managed to save it. She said that She encountered strong faith here in Medjugorje. This is all I know concerning these questions.

Did you understand Her intentions during the first days of the apparitions?

It was difficult to understand many things when I was a boy. I practiced religion, I was raised in a religious family, I prayed regularly, I was a good pupil at school and when I would get a C or D+ I was content. What I want to say is that I did not know anything about Her intentions. Sometimes I didn't even understand the messages She left. In the beginning I didn't feel comfortable and free enough to ask Gospa to explain Her words to me. In time, I started to understand what Her goal was. I understood what She wanted from us. I always tell people that my conversion did not happen over night. My conversion is a day-to-day process, it is what I aim for in life. It is a process for all of us. We must all decide to follow down the path of conversion, to decide to do good and cast aside the bad. In the morning when I wake up I think to myself *Mother, may whatever I do today be Your will, not mine. May it be Your will and the will of Your Son.* When I lay in bed at night I wonder, *Mother, do You approve of everything I did today?* I ask myself these questions every morning and every evening. During the time between two apparitions, I try to sieve and filter all that I do. I try to leave behind all that is bad and only let the good pass through. I will replace this sieve for a new one every single day because I want to be pure when I meet with Gospa. I know that She will not criticize me, She never does. She always teaches, advises and guides us with love. As human beings, there is a lot we can do on our own without Gospa telling us directly. We realize through prayer what needs to be done, what is good and what is not. We realize what we need to do in order for us to open our hearts to God.

You mentioned that you did not have any apparitions during the first ten days of your army service. Was there ever another time when you did not have an apparition?
I only did not have apparitions during the first ten days of my service. Gospa prepared me for this. I had apparitions later on and I was able to prepare for them, however, due to the conditions, the apparitions were short. After this I had a prayer meeting in Ljubljana and I was able to prepare for these apparitions in the same manner I prepare myself for them at home. This prayer meeting was held with the members of the Focolare. There were about thirty members present and they had their own house. I was able to pray regularly and I had regular apparitions there.

Did you have any uncomfortable situations while attending this meeting?
I never had any trouble. I did not notice anyone following me.

Where you allowed to go to church?
I did not go to church back then but we did have a priest there and I was able to attend Holy Mass.

Sometimes you have two apparitions a day?
Yes, I have been leading a prayer meeting for the last twenty eight years and our meetings take place every Monday

and Friday. I have two apparitions on these days, one at 6.40 PM and the second one at 22 PM, during the meeting.

The lives of visionaries are different from the lives of ordinary people. You meet with Gospa and testify about the apparitions on a daily basis... Over the past twenty nine years, did you ever think to yourself that your life would be much easier and simpler if you did not have this grace? In other words, do you consider what has happened to you a burden?
Not only is it not a burden, it is a great gift and brings me great joy. However, it also brings great responsibility. I know that God has given me so much but He also asks a lot of me. I am completely aware of the responsibility I have and I live with it every single day. As I have been living with Gospa for the past twenty nine years, trust me when I say that I am not afraid to die. I have seen everything and I know what awaits me in Heaven. Therefore, to me this earthly life is irrelevant and empty. To be with Gospa means to stand in the light which shines from Heaven and to see Heaven. It is not easy to come back to Earth after being in this light. I need time, sometimes up to a few hours, after each of my apparitions, to get used to reality and to accept this world. It is not easy at all.

How do you feel after an apparition ends?
At first, it is difficult to talk. People who are with me during my apparitions can see that my eyes are still closed when I convey Gospa's words to them. This happens after every apparition. Even when my apparition ends I am still with Her and it is difficult for me to return to this world. My eyes are still teary after an apparition; I still want to be with Gospa. I do not see Her but I wish to be with Her. It

is very difficult to explain and it is also difficult to describe an apparition; the time I spend with Gospa. It is impossible to describe the love of our Mother: when She looks at me during an apparition and when She looks at everyone else who is present. Sometimes I see tears of joy rolling down Her face; Her eyes and face are indescribably beautiful. On Thursday, there were a hundred and two priests present at the apparition, it was very special. It is always special when Gospa sees priests, Her loved ones. Gospa prays so much for Her shepherds; that they may look after their flock. As the Gospel tells us, and Gospa often repeats, if a sheep gets lost, the rest of the ninety-nine must be left in order to look for the lost one. Gospa tells us this and She prays for vocations to serve the Church. There will be no such vocations if we do not pray with our families. God calls for such vocations within a family and that is where priests are born.

How is it possible to pray with our families when there is so much confusion, so many broken marriages and broken homes in the world?

This is a grave problem. Statistically, every second or third marriage ends up in divorce. The pace of life has an impact on marriage and family. Gospa often repeats that the moral state of the world is catastrophic. There are many factors which influence this: the media, the internet and pornography. Modern technology is destroying the world. On the other hand, technology can have a positive influence and lead one into the right direction, onto the path of good. For example, the media, which has a negative impact on the world, can contribute to the spreading of Gospa's messages to the most distant parts of the world, to the loneliest people or families. Pope Benedict XVI stipulates that the Gospel needs to be spread through the media. The Church must also choose this means of communication for the joyful news to find its way to the hearts of people.

What can we do to help young people understand the values of marriage?

This is a very important question. Parents are no longer models for their children. All means of healthy communication and dialogue have disappeared between spouses. Each parent has their own approach towards a child or, too often, there is none at all. However, there are many healthy families which pray regularly. If you pray with your children and then one day you say that you do not have time for them, that you are too busy and that you have other commitments, you allow your child to go off course and to head into another direction. Gospa says, "Dear children, there are no holidays at the school of prayer, you need to pray everyday, on your own, as a family and a as a community." Many dream of entering into marriage but are not sufficiently prepared for it. They talk more about sex and other things and are not prepared for the arrival of their first child. They are not ready, they don't know what to do and don't know how to guide a child. They can't even change their diapers, let alone anything else.

Please describe what one of your days look like – from the time you get up in the morning till the time you go to bed at night.

I get up pretty early, especially during the summer, and then I climb Apparition Hill in silence. This means a great deal to me. It marks the beginning of a new day. Later, I return home and get ready for morning Mass. After Mass I have coffee with my brothers or friends. Then comes the time when I meet with pilgrims, with the ill and with priests. I have private meetings and talk with those who ask to meet with me. During the afternoon I leave time for myself: I read the Bible and dwell upon what I read. I think about what the words mean to me and what message they have for my life. The words from the Bible are meant for me, they talk to me. Having done this, I pray. After resting for a while, I make notes; as I do each day. These notes will come in handy once the apparitions stop taking place. They will help me remember my past experiences. When this is done, I prepare for my apparition after which I attend Adoration or some other prayer program, depending on the day of the week. Obviously, there are so many other things too; events that cannot be planned, such as meetings with the youth. Although I have a usual schedule, everyday is different.

In Her messages, Gospa repeats that we should "pray, pray, pray." How much time do you spend in prayer each day?

I try to pray at least three hours a day. I pray in the morning, at noon and in the evening, when it is most quiet.

How do you speak with Gospa? Can you talk to Her about your problems and hardships?

My conversations with Gospa are very casual. I speak to Her and She speaks to me. Other than giving me messages for the world and the Church, She nurtures and guides us. She guides me and gives advice for my family. She guides me, my family and my children; She advises me when I prepare for a trip: She tells me what to do, what to talk about and what parts of my speech to supplement. Gospa doesn't only do this for us visionaries, She wishes this for each and everyone of us.

Have you ever seen Gospa angry?

No, I have never seen Her angry. I have occasionally seen Her sad and I will tell you why. She is sad because of all the abortions, divorces and turmoil in the world. Through the last years She has been sad because of the events within the Church.

So, she is usually joyful?

Yes, most of the time She is happy.

Let's go back to 1981, when the apparitions first took place. You told us why the Queen of Peace chose the six of you, why She chose Bijakovići and the Parish of Medjugorje. In this context, I find it interesting that She chose children from a village situated in a communist country. The ideology of this communist country was to suppress religion and faith in God. Did you ever talk about this with Gospa?

I don't remember ever talking about this with Her. Whether the other visionaries have, I do not know.

In an effort to intimidate them the visionaries were interrogated, evaluated by psychiatrists and were even taken to morgues. Did you also experience such intimidation?

I was very shy as a child and, of course, I did experience some fear. On the third or forth day of the apparitions, I stopped feeling scared. I was ready to surrender my life for Gospa and the truth. Most of all, it was difficult to see my parents undergo ill-treatment. They were intimidated and threatened. When that didn't work, the authorities tried to bribe them to make us say that we fabricated the whole thing. Our parents were promised all sorts of riches if they managed to make us say that. It was also difficult because our parishioners were also taken in by police for interrogation and were later incarcerated. Although we were children at the time, it was hard because we knew that the parishioners were trying to protect us and that they were going through all of this because of us. Even though we knew they were innocent, it was agonizing for us to watch this.

You felt responsible for their ordeals even though you weren't.

Absolutely! We were under-age and therefore they could not torment us so they tormented the grown-ups.

A lot was written about the apparitions and the visionaries testify to them often. Nevertheless, in conversations with people, I'm always surprised when I find out that many people know little about this. There are people who ask questions such as whether you have daily apparitions. I'm not even sure that all of our parishioners know how many of the visionaries have daily apparitions. Please tell us something about how you prepare for an apparition, describe the apparition itself and how long it lasts.

Medjugorje has outgrown itself as a parish. Many have come here to open a business and not for spiritual renewal. Little of them or none at all know anything about the apparitions. Therefore, I would like to tell them as well as the parishioners who might have forgotten, because of the material pressure they feel, that we have apparitions everyday. We start to prepare ourselves for an apparition at 6PM and there is always a certain number of people present. We prepare by praying the Rosary together. As time passes and the moment of the apparition approaches, which is at 6.40 PM, I feel Gospa's presence more and more. The moment I kneel and stop praying is the moment when Gospa arrives. It is when I see a sign which Gospa comes with, it is the sign of light. Gospa doesn't appear at once. She comes gradually, in a beam of light. This light cannot be compared to any other light I know. It is the light of Heaven. I sometimes see Heaven behind this light. I see people walking, praying and singing. Faint music can also be heard. When Gospa appears I am no longer aware of my surroundings; I have no feeling for time or space. When She appears, She greets us in Her usual fashion with, "Praised be Jesus, my dear children." She sometimes addresses us by saying, "my little children."Gospa then prays over those who are present, over the ill and over the priests. When She finishes praying, Gospa and I talk. Sometimes the conversation is initiated by me and sometimes by Her. After we have talked, She blesses all those who are present with Her motherly love and then She blesses all objects brought to the apparition site. Then I recommend all those who are present at the apparition; I recommend their needs, wishes and illnesses. I also recommend those that have especially recommended themselves. Gospa intercedes for them before Her Son. She especially intercedes for the sick. Sometimes I ask Gospa questions which others have told me to ask. These questions usually come from the ill. When this is done, I have a private conversation with Gospa. The duration of our private conversations differ from apparition to apparition. When the apparition is over, Gospa leaves with a sign of a light and, greets us by saying, "Go in peace, my dear children."

The light that you mention, is it visible throughout the whole apparition?
Yes and Gospa never stands with Her feet on the ground. She always floats on a cloud.

What does She look like? Can you describe Her dress?
Her dress is grey and Her veil is white. She has blue eyes, rosy cheeks and black hair. She floats on a cloud and has a crown of stars above Her head. She dresses differently only for Christmas, Easter, the anniversary of the apparitions and on Her birthday. Instead of wearing Her grey dress, She wears a golden-colored one.

For how long do the apparitions last?
The longest apparition lasted for forty-five minutes, in 1983. The apparitions now last from five to fifteen minutes.

Does Gospa come alone?
Sometimes She is accompanied by angels. On Christmas, She comes with baby Jesus and St. Joseph. She comes like this during Midnight Mass.

Does St. Joseph ever talk?
No, he stands next to Her and joyfully gazes upon Her.

Does She hold baby Jesus in Her arms?
Yes. As I am always in a kneeling position, I only see one side of His face.

Are baby Jesus' eyes open?
Yes, His eyes are open and He smiles. Two years ago, my wife and children were with me at Midnight Mass. I took my children's hands and laid them on baby Jesus. The looks in my children's eyes were special.

Did your children feel that they were touching Jesus?
Yes.

The thirtieth anniversary of the first apparition is approaching. Much is said about the messages. Can you, nonetheless, tell us what the principal messages from Gospa are?

I would like to emphasize the main messages, the core messages with which Gospa has lead us since 1981. These messages are messages of peace, conversion, returning to God, placing God first, heading to the future with Him, praying with our hearts, penance and fasting, strong faith, love, forgiveness, the Eucharist and the message of hope. Gospa leads us with these messages. She simplifies them for us so that we can understand them and live by them. The messages Gospa gives us on the 25th of each month simplify and explain the ones I have mentioned. These messages are messages of the Gospel. Jesus, Her Son, sends Her to us so that She can lead us. There is no other path to be followed but this one.

Many people say that the messages are simple and many pilgrims say that Gospa should leave new messages for us everyday. I wonder whether we would be able follow such a torrent of messages? Are we competent enough to follow the message Gospa gave us yesterday and are we ready for a new one today? Back in 1984, Gospa left messages for the parish and the world on every Thursday. She continued to do so for the next three years. She realized that a week was not enough time for the messages to be comprehended and therefore decided to leave messages every month instead. She gave us more time to think about them and to start living by them. She knows what to do, She is a teacher. As Cardinal Schoenborn said, Gospa is the greatest pastoral worker of our time. This is so true.

According to some estimates, about forty million pilgrims have visited Medjugorje so far. In August of 2010,

325 000 Holy Communions were handed out. This is something that has never happened before. One question rises here: do we, the parishioners as well as believers from all around the world understand why Gospa has come?

This is a very good question which concerns me as well because I, too, often wonder if I have completely understood Gospa. I hope that I have but I also know that I have to work on this more. People come looking for a spring, they come to this spring and they quench their thirsty souls at this spring. They return home restored. In order for us to understand the messages, we need to be wise within our souls. We need to pray more and then we shall find the answer to this question and understand it within our hearts.

Ivan, you see Gospa every single day. Can you describe Her for us?

She cannot be described with words. No matter how long I search for the right words, each word is poor in description. It is impossible to describe Her love, smile, warmth and tenderness. It is especially hard to describe the love that She has for us. It is merely impossible. I have tried to describe Her but my description is insufficient. She cannot be described with human words.

Many artists have tried to paint images or make sculptures of Her. Have they ever come close enough to truly portraying Her?

It is impossible to describe Her even to artists. Some of the paintings and sculptures that were created according to our descriptions portray a little bit of Her, but do not even come close enough to depicting Her.

There have been many negative reactions in connection to the visionaries from the very first day of the apparitions. Many have said that this is a hoax or a result of hallucinations... We often hear or read of such statements even today. Does this bother you?

It bothers me when it comes from within the Church or from a priest, particularly when such statements are not backed up with well thought out arguments. If they were then I would be able to understand. When I think about this I don't understand why such people do not have patience where this is concerned. Why aren't they willing to wait for the Church's ruling on this matter? On the other hand, when I remember how Jesus had lived on Earth and performed miracles, His disciples, who witnessed everything Jesus did, still denounced Him. Lucky are those who do not see yet believe.

Have you ever contemplated this with Gospa? Did you ever ask, "How can I convince those who do not believe?" Did you ever ask Her what to do so that people may start believing?

No, Gospa does not speak of such things. All She asks of us is that we pray. To believe is truly a gift. People who come from all corners of the world to Medjugorje do not need to be convinced. As soon as they arrive they feel Her presence, they see the fruits of Her teachings and understand what She wants from us. It is important to open our hearts and to accept what God offers. It is important that we stand before the cross with our families. This is when we shall receive many graces.

Those who have received graces in Medjugorje say that the only important thing is simply to come here, the rest will be taken care of by Gospa.

That is the first step. Whoever has taken that first step has received grace.

You have undergone all kinds of medical examinations performed by renowned experts from all over the world. Yes, we went through all sorts of examinations and tests, conducted in Milano and Vienna. We also went through such examination in Medjugorje, also performed by experts. I went through all this even though I found it difficult particularly because some if these tests were repeated up to four times. Nevertheless, we agreed to do them because Gospa advised us to.

Does this mean you have spoken with Her about these examinations and tests? Yes, we have talked about this. I asked Her whether or not I should go through with them. We agreed that I should because this was what the Church wanted. All these results are carefully looked after and have been forwarded to the International Committee founded by the Vatican. I believe they will greatly influence the rulings and decisions of the Church. Gospa told us to accept these examinations and that we shall understand later why they were important.

We are approaching the end of this meeting and I hope that we shall have many more fruitful interviews. To concluded, every visionary has his or her own special intention for which they pray. You pray for the youth and for families. What is the essence of the intentions you pray for? It is my mission to pray for the youth, families and priests. My intentions were presented to me by Gospa. I pray for this everyday and I also have a prayer group which prays with me. We have been praying together for the last twenty - eight years. We meet every Monday and Friday. Whenever I take part in a prayer meeting anywhere in the world, I always especially ask to meet with the youth, and if necessary, with their parents too. These meetings are always very fruitful. This is how I directly pass Gospa's messages onto the youth. However critical we are towards the youth and their way of life, there are always more and more young people who come to Medjugorje, especially during the Youth Festival. It gives me great joy when I see so many young people in Medjugorje.

Just one more thing... What is your advice to those of us who live in Medjugorje?

First and foremost – we need to be responsible. The time we live in is a time of responsibility and we need to become responsible individuals and responsible when Gospa's message are at hand. We should be responsible in accepting Her messages, in weaving them into our lives and in being living examples. People often ask me when will Gospa leave a sign...She will leave a sign. However, today, we need to be those signs. This parish must be a sign. The youth in Medjugorje must be a sign. Our families must be living signs for all the pilgrims that come here, the whole world must be a living sign – this is what the word 'responsibility' means. We must all be responsible – you and I, the parish as well as the priests who do pastoral work here. We need to be responsible and act not according to what the world says, but to what the Gospel says - what Gospa invites us to.

Vicka Ivanković-Mijatović

Vicka Ivanković-Mijatović was born on September 3, 1964, in Bijakovići. She has had daily apparitions since June 24, 1981. She has been entrusted with nine secrets. Along with her husband Mario and their children Marija Sofija and Ante, she lives in Krehin Gradac, near Medjugorje. Her prayer intention is to pray for the sick.

MEDJUGORJE HAS BECOME IMPORTANT THROUGH THE MESSAGES OF OUR LADY

Please, Vicka, describe for us the feelings a person has, who has been having daily meetings with the Mother of God for so many years.
No words can describe this feeling. It is something unique, a special peace, contentment, a joy that can only be experienced when one is with the Gospa.

Have you ever asked the Gospa why She had chosen the six of you from Bijakovići?
Before the apparitions, I never even dreamt that this would happen. We asked the Gospa this question and She said that this was the will of God, not Hers.

What does the Gospa wish of the visionaries?
She wishes us to be the true bearers of Her messages.

What does She expect of other people?
Her main messages are that man decides for prayer, for conversion, for fasting, for penance and for peace. This is what we need to decide for and to live accordingly, this is what the Gospa wishes of us. The Gospa does not expect anything extraordinary. She explains that She is not here to bring new messages, to tell us something new. She is here to wake us up, because we have fallen asleep and have wan-

dered away from God. There is nothing new in the messages; we only have to live according to the Bible.

What do you admire most about the Gospa?

I cannot single out anything in particular. Every meeting with the Gospa is so wonderful as if it happened for the first time. I never expect anything special. However, since we are mentioning details, I can say that it is magnificent to see the Gospa at Christmas when She appears with baby Jesus in Her arms. Once on Good Friday, She appeared with the adult Jesus. He was covered with wounds, with torn garments and had a crown of thorns on His head. The Gospa said: *"I came so that you may see what Jesus suffered for all of us."* I have seen Him as a baby and at the moment of His suffering, especially the moment of His death. I single this out because it concerns Jesus. As far as the Gospa is concerned, I cannot single out anything because Her appearances are simply sublime.

Does the Queen of Peace appear as a woman from our distant past or is She a woman of our time?

Personally, I see and experience Her as a woman of our time, so as if She were living in the present time.

Do you think that people are living the messages?

On one occasion, the Gospa said that there are people who accept the messages and who start living them, but then, suddenly, they seem to get tired. The Gospa says that She would prefer if we accepted one message with our heart and took one step at a time, without stopping. People quickly accept everything and then they come to a sudden stop. We need to slowly accept the messages and take them into our life and pray; in this way, we shall not get tired so quickly, of course, only if we accept them with the heart.

How is it possible for people not only to hear the messages, but also to accept them?

We do know how to hear and accept the messages. The only problem is that we turn to the messages only if we have a problem, but God also makes use of this to be closer to man.

During the second apparition, the Gospa said that She was the Queen of Peace. One of the main messages and invitations to man is the call to peace. How did you understand this call to peace as a girl, considering that in 1981 there was no war in this region and in Europe?

I would like to correct you. During the second apparition, the Gospa said: *"I am the Blessed Virgin Mary,"* and then, a few days later, She said: *"I am the Queen of Peace and I have come to bring you peace."* Yes, at that time, it was rather quiet in Europe and I did not understand what She meant by this. However, in Her messages, She constantly repeated: *"Pray for peace", "With prayer and fasting even wars can be stopped."* Occasionally, we would hear that some wars broke out, for example in Iraq or Iran, but we hardly knew where these places were.

Then, one day, war broke out here at home. The Gospa told us that She had already been with us for ten years and that, with Her messages, She had given us the opportunity to help Her avoid this war. But unfortunately, we had not taken Her call seriously.

Often other people are also present during your apparitions. How does the Gospa look upon a sinner and how does She look upon you?

The Gospa makes no difference between, as you put it, a sinner and me. The Gospa hopes that the sinner will convert that he will come back. Possibly, She might love him even more and give him more love than She gives me, because She wishes to save him and free him of sin.

What fascinates you most during an apparition?
Maybe the feeling of no longer being on earth, as if I was floating in air.

You have also been entrusted with secrets. What is it like to live with these secrets?
The Gospa has so far entrusted me with nine of the ten secrets. This is not difficult for me at all because, when She gave me the secrets, She also gave me the strength to live with them. I live my life as if the secrets did not exist.

Do you know when you will receive the tenth secret?
I don't know.

Do you know when you will be able to reveal the secrets?
I don't know this either.

Do you sometimes think about the secrets?
Sure, I think about them, because they contain a piece of future; but this is no burden for me.

The Gospa has spoken of Her life with you. Can you reveal any of it now?
The Gospa has told me about Her entire life, from birth to ascension. At the moment, I cannot talk about this as I have not yet received permission. I have written down Her biog-

raphy in three notebooks, in which I wrote down what She told me. I would sometimes write one page, sometimes two and sometimes just half a page, depending on how much I could remember.

In other places, the apparitions usually have not lasted for such a long time, some of them for only a few days. In Medjugorje, they have been going on for years.

Yes. Once we asked Her for how long She would stay and She answered: *"Have you grown tired of me already?"* Since then, we have never asked Her this again. The Gospa has also told us that She will complete in Medjugorje what She had started in Fatima.

How do you feel during the apparitions? In comparison with the first apparitions, has anything changed?

Nothing has changed. These meetings are always the same for me. I prepare myself with prayer and then prayer defines every apparition which is about to happen. The more I pray, the more I prepare myself, the more I am ready for the meeting.

How do you speak with the Gospa? Is it an informal conversation?

I speak with Her as I speak with you, completely free – there is no difference.

Have you ever spoken with Her about the future of the apparitions?

No, I have not. She will speak of this on Her own. When there is something important to speak about, the Gospa will speak of it Herself. There is no need for me to ask.

During the first days of the apparitions, you and the rest of the visionaries spoke of a sign that the Gospa promised to leave on Apparition Hill. Has anything regarding this sign changed? Will there really be a sign?

Nothing has changed. This is the third of the secrets, which the Gospa has entrusted us with. She will leave a sign on the site of the apparition, it will be permanent, visible and indestructible.

You have seen the sign?

Yes, I saw it once.

How can we reconcile what the Gospa asks of us in Her messages with the rhythm of our way of life?

Today we live very fast, we need to slow down. If we carry on living like this and at this pace, we shall not get anywhere. We should never think, "I must! I must!" God in His wisdom will take care of everything. The problem lies within us, we are the ones who set the pace of our life. If I tell myself to go slowly, then the world will change. It is not God's fault, it is our fault. We have set the pace for ourselves and so we think that we cannot live any other way.

What prayers does the Queen of Peace recommend most?

She mostly recommends the rosary, this is Her favorite prayer - the Joyful, the Sorrowful and the Glorious Mysteries. But the Gospa says that every prayer that is prayed with the heart and with love is just as valuable. To pray a single Hail Mary with your heart is worth more than three rosaries that are prayed carelessly.

What does the Gospa expect of us now?
The same that She expected from the very beginning. There are always people who have just begun and those who are taking the next step forward. Therefore, the Gospa expects the same: Do it!

What significance does Medjugorje have in the world?
Medjugorje is of great importance. Not as a place, but Medjugorje as a message. It is something that man cannot comprehend. The messages of Our Lady have spread all over the world, to all corners of the earth. Considering the messages and letters I receive from all over the world, people are enthusiastic. This place has become an oasis of peace. Nowhere else can one find more peace than here under the safeguard of Our Lady, in Her presence under Her mantle. This is why this is so. Medjugorje is of great importance because of the messages of Our Lady, because She is still here and because Her presence can be expected daily. Lourdes, Fatima and other places of apparitions are beautiful and it is wonderful to be there, but it is a different feeling when the Gospa is present and not a thing of the past. Medjugorje is important because people feel that here Heaven is on earth, because the Gospa is here every day.
One cannot compare this with anything, one cannot describe in words the meaning of Medjugorje. For those, who come to Medjugorje, Medjugorje is holy ground.

The visionaries are witnesses but, at the same time, they are responsible for the spreading of the messages of the Gospa. Also we, who have understood the message, are responsible for their being spread. How can we spread these messages?

Everyone is invited to live and spread the messages just like the visionaries have been chosen by God to spread the messages to people. The Gospa says that She is happy about every pilgrim who comes to Medjugorje. But She is even more joyous when a pilgrim accepts the messages in his heart, lives them and, through his life and example, spreads them to others.

At the beginning of the apparitions, the visionaries had problems with the authorities. However, even today, there are those who condescendingly smile at everything that has happened in Medjugorje since June 24, 1981. Is it hard for you when you meet such people?
Neither I nor the other visionaries had problems with the authorities; the authorities had their problems with us. As far as we are concerned, I can say that we never did anything bad, we didn't bother anybody but this bothered the authorities. We always remained calm and told the authorities what I tell you now or what I have been telling everyone since 1981. It is their problem that they did not wish to accept our words.

Those who ridicule the messages and the apparitions, ridicule themselves – this does not concern us. They also have the opportunity to convert in these times.

You meet the Gospa every day, this means that you are in contact with Heaven so to say. Can you compare this life with the life that awaits us in Heaven?
The Gospa says that we can live Heaven, hell or Purgatory already here on earth, depending on what a person decides for. She also says that many think that everything is over when one dies. But the Gospa confirms that we are merely temporarily here on earth and that we can never compare earthly life with what awaits us in Heaven.

OUR LADY'S SCHOOL OF PRAYER

The most important messages of Our Lady are **prayer, conversion, fasting, penance** and **peace.** That is why Our Lady recommends that we pray the Joyous, Sorrowful and Glorious Mysteries of the Rosary every day. On Wednesdays and Fridays, we should fast on bread and water. But most important of all, our faith must be strong.

When Our Lady asks us to pray, She does not wish us to pray only with words, She wants us to open our hearts more and more every day so that prayer will truly become joy. Our Lady also says that, before we start to pray, we should get rid of all thoughts that bother us by praying an **Our Father**. She also says: **"Pray to your almighty Father in Heaven, who is full of immeasurable love, who loves us so much, and give Him all your wishes and all your problems. Allow Him to transform everything for the best, that His will may be done, not ours."**

The next day, we shall add a **Hail Mary;** let us greet our Mother, whom we see with the eyes of our heart, who is always close to us and who loves us so much. The day after tomorrow, we shall add a **Glory Be** and so honor our Father. We should be grateful for everything that He gives us, for the good and the bad, so that we may comprehend that everything comes from Him.

In this way, our heart will open more every day and we will think about the words we speak; this is how we will learn the meaning of these words and how to live them.

A Flower Cannot Survive Without Water and We Cannot Survive Without God's Mercy

Our Lady gave us a very good example by comparing this with a plant we have in our home. If we water this plant with a few drops of water every day, it will grow and, finally, a beautiful flower will emerge. It is the same with our heart. If we plant two or three words of prayer into our heart each day, our heart will grow and blossom like that plant. But if we forget to water the plant for several days, it will wither and disappear as if it had never existed.

Our Lady says that this is also how it is with us. When the time comes to pray, we often say that we are tired or that we have other "more important" things to take care of, and so we say that we will pray tomorrow. This goes on for days; instead of prayer, other worldly and bad things enter into our heart. Therefore, Our Lady says: **"As a plant cannot live without water so too we cannot live without God's mercy."**

She teaches us that praying with the heart cannot be learned by studying, but only through prayer, by taking one step forward each day.

When Our Lady asks us also to fast, She does not ask those who are ill not to eat, She asks them to give up, for that day, what they like to eat most. Those, who are healthy but say that they cannot fast because they don't feel well or because they get a head-ache, She tells that they should develop a strong will.

An Invitation to Conversion Throughout the World

Our Lady invites us all to convert. She says: **"Dear children, when you have problems, difficulties and troubles, you always think that Jesus and I are far from you. No, we are always close to you, just open your hearts so that you may see with your hearts how much we love you."**

She also asks us to give up something that we like most. She would be most happy if we don't commit sins. Therefore, Our Lady says: **"I give you my peace and my love so that you may give them to your families, neighbors and friends."** She gives us Her peace, Her blessings and She prays for all of us.

Our Lady would be overjoyed if the rosary were renewed within our families and communities, if parents and children prayed together so that Satan could not harm us. Our Lady emphasizes how strong Satan is and that he wishes to harm us in everything. This is why She calls us to pray more so that we can resist his temptations with prayer. We can do this best by praying the rosary because the rosary is the strongest weapon in the fight against Satan.

Our Lady recommends that we always carry a blessed object with us – a small cross, a medal, or some small sign to defend ourselves against Satan.

May Holy Mass Be in the First Place

Our Lady teaches us that Holy Mass should come first, that this is the most important and most holy moment, as the living Jesus comes and we accept Him in our heart. She wishes us to prepare for Mass seriously so that we could accept Jesus with dignity and love. She also recommends monthly confession. She tells us not to comprehend holy confession as a means of freeing us from our sins and then continue to live our lives the way we did before. She wants us to change and become new persons. She also says that during confession we should ask the priest for advice so that we may progress one step further.

We Live in a Time of Special Grace

Our Lady is especially worried about the youth throughout the world. They find themselves in a very difficult situation.

They can only be helped with our love and our prayers with the heart. For this reason, Our Lady says: **"Dear youngsters, what today's world offers you is temporary and it is through these things that you can see how Satan seizes every moment for himself. Today, he mostly throws himself onto the youth and he wishes to destroy our families."** This is why Our Lady wants us to be carriers of Her peace. But first we must pray for peace in our hearts, in our families and in our communities so that together we may pray for peace in the world. She says that if we pray for peace in the world but we do not have peace within our hearts, then prayer is not very useful.

Heaven, Purgatory and Hell

Jakov and I received a special gift. Our Lady took us along with Her and showed us **Heaven, hell** and **purgatory**. We were at Jakov's house and suddenly Our Lady came and told us that we are going to go with Her. Jakov said: *"Dear Gospa, please take Vicka instead of me. She has more brothers and sisters, I am an only child."* Jakov thought that we were going to leave and never come back. At this moment, I thought of how many hours or days it would take and whether we would go upwards towards Heaven or downwards into earth... Our Lady took me by my right arm, Jakov by his left and took us with Her.

In less than second, we were in **Heaven**, in an endless space. We saw a light that does not exist on earth. We saw people dressed in various colors, grey, pink and yellow dresses. People walked around, prayed and sang, small angels circling above them. Our Lady then said to us: **"Look how happy people in Heaven are."** We saw joy, which cannot be described, a type of joy that does not exist on earth.

Purgatory is also an immense space, but one cannot see people there, dusk prevails, an ash-grey atmosphere. One can feel figures shivering, twitching, lashing out, moaning. They urgently need our prayers so that they may be freed from purgatory.

In the middle of **hell**, there is a fire. We saw people in their normal state and we saw how they looked later. Later, they emerged from the fire resembling various animals, as if they had never been human beings. The deeper they fall into the fire, the more they rebel against God. Our Lady told us that people, who are in hell, have gone there by their own will, because they wanted to. These are people who, while on earth, did everything against the will of God, they already lived hell on earth and this life continues here in hell. Our Lady also said that many people believe that life on earth is everything. To the contrary, on earth we are just passing through, life continues after life.

I Am Beautiful Because I Love

Before Our Lady appears to us, we see a light three times. This is the sign that She is coming. She is dressed in a grey dress, a white veil and She has a crown of stars above Her head. She has blue eyes, black hair and rosy cheeks. She floats in air on a grey cloud, She never touches the ground. On the eve before great feast days like Easter, Christmas, the Assumption of the Blessed Virgin Mary, Her birthday – She appears in a golden dress. At Christmas, She comes with little baby Jesus in Her arms. Once, a few years ago, on Good Friday, She came with the adult Jesus. He was covered with wounds and had a thorn crown on His head. But this was only once. Our Lady then said: **"I have come with Jesus so that you may see how much He suffered for all."**

Our Lady appears as a living person – like we are, but Her beauty can not be described because there is nothing as beautiful as She is. Once we asked Our Lady why She was so beautiful and She said: **"I am beautiful because I love. Start loving so that you too may be beautiful. This beauty does not come from without but from within our hearts and souls."** She says that we concern ourselves too much with outer beauty and so forget the beauty of the heart and soul. For this reason, She asks us to preoccupy ourselves more with the beauty of the heart and soul because, once we posses this beauty, our outer beauty will become apparent too.

THE SIGN BEFORE
THE APPARITIONS

The Two Rosaries
A few weeks before the first apparition took place, something strange occurred on Podbrdo that no one could explain.

One morning, on his way to fetch wood from Medovice, Vicka's ten-year-old brother Franjo, found two rosaries in the corner of the trailer attached to a motor vehicle, which they were supposed to use that day to fetch wood. One rosary was somewhat larger with wooden beads and had a wooden cross with the stations of the cross imprinted on its back. The other rosary was made of carob seeds, often seen in these parts.

Surprised, Franjo took these rosaries home. The neighbors and people of the village were asked if someone had forgotten them and left them there. But the answers were all negative. Nobody knew anything about these rosaries.

When the apparitions began, Vicka's grandmother told her to ask the Gospa where the rosaries had come from.
The Gospa answered: *"These rosaries are my special gift to your family."*

CONTENTS